MACM
INTERI

SIR ARTHUR CONAN DOYLE

The Norwood Builder
and Other Stories

Retold by F H Cornish

MACMILLAN

MACMILLAN READERS

INTERMEDIATE LEVEL

Founding Editor: John Milne

The Macmillan Readers provide a choice of enjoyable reading materials for learners of English. The series is published at six levels – Starter, Beginner, Elementary, Pre-intermediate, Intermediate and Upper.

Level Control

Information, structure and vocabulary are controlled to suit the students' ability at each level.

The number of words at each level:

Starter	about 300 basic words
Beginner	about 600 basic words
Elementary	about 1100 basic words
Pre-intermediate	about 1400 basic words
Intermediate	about 1600 basic words
Upper	about 2200 basic words

Vocabulary

Some difficult words and phrases in this book are important for understanding the story. Some of these words are explained in the story, some are shown in the pictures and others are marked with a number like this: …[3]. Phrases are marked with [P]. Words with a number are explained in the *Glossary* at the end of the book and phrases are explained on the *Useful Phrases* pages.

Answer Keys

Answer Keys for the *Points For Understanding* and *Exercises* sections can be found at www.macmillanenglish.com/readers.

Audio Download

There is an audio download available to buy for this title. Visit www.macmillanenglish.com/readers for more information.

Contents

A Note About The Author

Arthur Ignatius Conan Doyle was born in Edinburgh, the capital city of Scotland. He was born on 22nd May 1859 and he was the third of his parents' nine children. His father, Charles Doyle, was a government official who was also quite a successful artist. But Charles became seriously ill and life at home was difficult for the children. Because of this, young Arthur lived at his school for most of each year.

As he grew up, young Arthur decided to become a doctor. He studied medicine at Edinburgh University, where one of his teachers was Dr Joseph Bell. Arthur greatly admired Bell and his methods for finding out what people's problems really were.

When he left university, Conan Doyle moved to England. In 1882, he began to work as a family doctor in Southsea, on the south coast. In 1885, he married Louise Hawkins, the daughter of one of his patients. Conan Doyle did not really enjoy working as a family doctor and he soon moved to London with his family. Conan Doyle was especially interested in eyes and their problems, and he wanted to work in that area of medicine. But he had also begun to write fiction in his spare time. At first he wrote ghost stories and historical novels – stories about the past – but he did not have much success with these. Then in 1887, he published[1] a novel set in his own time. The novel was called *A Study in Scarlet*, and it was about a detective called Sherlock Holmes. Holmes was a man with no emotions[2] but with a very logical[3] mind. Holmes's methods for solving[4] problems were based[5] on Conan Doyle's memories of his university teacher, Dr Bell.

The novel was a great success, and Conan Doyle stopped working as a doctor in 1888. He concentrated on writing about Sherlock Holmes. There was another novel-length story – *The Sign of Four*, published in 1889 – but most of the detective's adventures appeared as short stories. These stories were first published in a popular monthly magazine, *The Strand Magazine*. When Conan Doyle had written enough of these short stories, they were republished as collections in books. The first two collections were *The Adventures of Sherlock Holmes* (1892) and *The Memoirs of Sherlock Holmes* (1894).

In 1894, Conan Doyle decided that he preferred to write his historical novels. In the last story of *The Memoirs of Sherlock Holmes*, it seemed that the detective had been killed in Switzerland. Conan Doyle wrote no more Holmes stories for about ten years and he tried to forget about his detective. But his readers wanted to read more about Holmes, and in 1903 Conan Doyle published a further Holmes novel, *The Hound of the Baskervilles*. This story is about an earlier adventure of Holmes's, before his death. Conan Doyle still thought that he had killed his detective, but his readers were not happy about this. So, in 1905, Conan Doyle published a new short-story collection, *The Return of Sherlock Holmes*. Holmes had *not* died in Switzerland. He was alive and still solving problems.

Conan Doyle had been given a knighthood in 1902 – he became Sir Arthur Conan Doyle. In 1906, Conan Doyle's wife, Louise, died after being ill for many years, and in 1907 he married again. His second wife, Jean Leckie, had been his friend for a long time. He lived with her for the rest of his life in a large country house. Conan Doyle had a daughter and a son from his first marriage, and he had two sons and a daughter with Jean.

Conan Doyle went on writing his historical stories in these years, as well as some non-fiction books about the histories of various wars. He also wrote several science-fiction stories about a scientist called Professor Challenger. In the first of these – a novel called *The Lost World* (1912) – Challenger and his friends discover a place where dinosaurs still live. There are three Challenger novels and two short stories about him.

Conan Doyle also published more collections of Holmes short stories, as well as a fourth Holmes novel. The novel was *The Valley of Fear* (1915). The short stories appeared in *His Last Bow* (1917) and *The Casebook of Sherlock Holmes* (1927).

After a busy life, Sir Arthur Conan Doyle died on 7th July 1930. His body was buried in the garden of his country house, although[6] many years later it was moved to a churchyard.

Since Conan Doyle's death, several other writers have written stories about Sherlock Holmes. There have also been many films made from the Holmes stories. A famous series of Holmes films in the 1940s starred Basil Rathbone. Much more recently, Robert Downey Junior has appeared as the detective in two films directed by Guy Ritchie.

Other Sherlock Holmes books in the Macmillan Readers series include: *The Hound of the Baskervilles*, *The Sign of Four*, *Silver Blaze and Other Stories*, and *The Speckled Band and Other Stories*. *The Lost World* is also available. Visit the Macmillan Readers website at www.macmillanenglish.com/readers for more details.

A Note About The Stories

The four stories in this book are taken from three different collections of Sherlock Holmes stories. *The Norwood Builder* and *The Second Stain* were published in *The Return of Sherlock Holmes*; *The Stockbroker's Clerk* was published in *The Memoirs of Sherlock Holmes*; and *A Scandal in Bohemia* was published in *The Adventures of Sherlock Holmes*.

Sir Arthur Conan Doyle wrote the Sherlock Holmes stories in the voice of Holmes's friend and helper, Dr John H. Watson – he is the narrator. Watson tells us that the cases[7] he is publishing are only a small percentage of the hundreds of cases that Holmes has investigated[8] with his help. The stories do not appear in date order within the collections. Each book contains stories from different times in Holmes's career. Some stories are set as early as the 1880s, and one of the later stories happens during World War I (1914–18). In some stories, Watson is an unmarried man who shares an apartment at 221b Baker Street, London, with Holmes. In other stories, Watson is a married man, living in his own house, who helps his friend from time to time. In later stories, Watson's wife has died and he is living with Holmes again. Watson is obviously[9] not as clever as Holmes – Conan Doyle makes this clear. In each investigation, the narrator is given the same information as Holmes, but he can never understand what it really means. But Watson is strong and fearless. Holmes likes him and needs him as a helper.

The middle of the nineteenth century was a great period for railway building in Britain. At the time that the earliest Holmes stories take place, it was easy to get from one town to another by train. But there were no cars at that time, and Holmes and Watson often have to use cabs to move around central London. These two-wheeled cabs were pulled by horses, and so were the four-wheeled carriages which rich people often used.

There were also no telephones at the time of the earlier stories, but it was easy to send telegrams. As the railways were built, telegraph wires were put up beside the railway tracks. You could write a message and take it to a post office. There, the message was changed into a code[10] which was sent along the telegraph wires electronically. Very quickly, the coded message arrived at a post office near the home of the person you wanted to contact. Then it was changed back into a written form and was delivered to the home of the person that it was addressed to. The written message was usually delivered by a boy, on foot or on a bicycle. Telegrams arrived much sooner than letters sent by post. Holmes receives several telegrams in these stories, and he receives them very soon after they are sent.

People sent letters too. At the time of these stories, it was very common for letters, as well as legal[11] papers, to be sealed[12] with wax. Wax is a solid substance which melts when it is heated. If you wanted to seal a letter, you melted some sealing wax on the envelope. You used the flame of a candle to melt the wax, which quickly became solid again on the envelope. Then no one could open the envelope without breaking the piece of wax, and showing that the letter had been opened and read. People often pressed a finger-ring into the wax. The ring would have a design in it which would leave an impression in the wax. Each person could have their own design – perhaps their initials – on their ring, so the person receiving the letter knew who it was from. Sealing wax is used in one of the stories in this book to mislead the police.

Another dishonest use for wax is described in this book too – key copying. If you wanted to copy a key to open a lock that you should not open, you could make an impression of the key in wax. You needed only to borrow the key secretly for a few seconds. Then a special metalworker called a locksmith could pour liquid metal into the impression. When the metal was solid again, you would have a new key.

At the time of these stories, and for many years after, there were very hard punishments for crimes. The death penalty was the usual punishment for murder in Britain. Murderers who were sentenced to death were executed – they were killed in a prison.

Dr Watson's Introduction

My name is John Watson and I am a doctor. For many years I was a doctor in the British Army, but one day I was shot in the shoulder and badly hurt. After that, I left the army. It was then that I met a man named Mr Sherlock Holmes. Holmes and I quickly became friends and for several years we shared a flat in Baker Street, near Regent's Park in London.

Holmes is an extraordinary man. He has a very logical mind. And this mind is like a great book of knowledge – an encyclopaedia. Holmes knows about hundreds of different things. He is a scientist – he has published many articles about science. He is also a musician – he plays the violin well and he has published articles on music too. But above all, he knows about crime and criminals. Holmes is a consulting[13] detective and all kinds of people consult him. Sometimes the cases he investigates are crimes. Sometimes they are personal problems. Holmes is an independent detective – he does not work for the police. Sometimes the detectives at Scotland Yard – the London police headquarters – consult him themselves, and then he works *with* them. But sometimes he works for people the police have arrested[14]. Then he works *against* the police.

Holmes investigates any case that he finds really interesting. The more difficult the puzzle[15], the more Holmes enjoys it. As I said, Holmes is an extraordinary man, and for a number of years I have been this extraordinary man's assistant. I will not say that my mind is like Holmes's mind, but I always try to understand his methods. I have worked with him on many cases, and I have always written about these cases when we have finished our investigations. From time to time, I publish these records, and this book contains four of them.

THE NORWOOD BUILDER

1

The Most Unhappy Man

The case which I call 'The Norwood Builder' began for us in a very dramatic way. Holmes and I had just finished a late breakfast one morning, and we were talking in our sitting room in Baker Street. Holmes was about to open his morning newspaper, when we heard a lot of noise outside. A moment later, someone was knocking at the door, very hard. Then the door opened and a young man rushed[16] in. His face was pale and his fair hair and his clothes were untidy. His blue eyes were frightened. He had obviously been running, and he was breathing heavily.

'You've got to help me, Mr Holmes,' he said desperately[17]. 'The police are following me! Oh, the scandal[18] will break my poor mother's heart[P].'

'Sit down, please,' Holmes said. 'This is my friend and helper, Dr Watson. Please tell us who *you* are.'

'I'm that most unhappy man, John Hector McFarlane,' he replied. He obviously thought that we would recognize the name, but we did not.

'Mr Holmes, if the police arrive, please make them wait,' the young man went on. 'Don't let them arrest me until I've told you my story.'

'Why do they want to arrest you?' asked Holmes in surprise. 'What crime will they charge[19] you with?'

'They'll charge me with murder, Mr Holmes, but I haven't killed anyone,' he replied. 'But I will be happy to go to prison if I know that Sherlock Holmes is investigating my case!'

Holmes is a tall, thin man with long fingers and a long

neck. His eyes are like a fierce[20] bird's eyes. Now he looked very carefully at our visitor.

'I know that you're not married and that you're a lawyer,' said Holmes. 'I know that your lungs[21] are not good. But I know nothing else about you, and I do *not* recognize your name.'

I knew my friend's methods, and I could understand what he was thinking. The man's clothes were untidy, so he was probably unmarried. We could see that there were legal papers in his pockets, so he was certainly a lawyer. We could hear his heavy breathing, so it was obvious that he had an illness of the lungs. Everything that Holmes had said was obvious, but the young man seemed surprised.

'That's amazing,' he said. 'But if you'd opened your newspaper this morning, you would have recognized my name.'

The man opened the newspaper which Holmes had put on the table and pointed dramatically to a headline. Then he held the paper up so we could both see it.

MYSTERIOUS CRIME COMMITTED IN NORWOOD! A WELL-KNOWN BUILDER IS MISSING. THE POLICE THINK THAT HE HAS BEEN MURDERED AND THEY ARE SEARCHING[22] FOR A SUSPECT[23].

'And I *am* the suspect,' our visitor said.

'Your case sounds interesting,' said Holmes, looking very pleased. 'Watson, please read the newspaper article.'

I read what was in front of me.

Mr Jonas Oldacre, from the district[24] of Norwood, has disappeared. The police suspect that he has been murdered. Mr Oldacre is a man in his fifties who has lived in Norwood, on the southern edge of London, for many years. He owns a building firm[25] there. Recently he seems to have stopped working as a builder and he rarely meets anyone. Mr Oldacre lives alone except for[26] an elderly woman who is his housekeeper[27]. Yesterday evening, he was visited at home by Mr John Hector McFarlane, a lawyer who works in central London. Then, very early this morning, a fire was discovered in a timber store[28] behind Mr Oldacre's house. All the wood in the store was burnt. But when the firemen had put out the flames, no one could find Mr Oldacre. He had not slept in his bed, and a safe[29] which he kept in his bedroom had been opened. The police found some blood in the bedroom and they also found a heavy walking stick, which belongs to Mr McFarlane. There was some blood on the walking stick too.

A door leading from Mr Oldacre's bedroom to the garden was open. There were some marks[30] on the ground outside it which led towards the timber store. The police think that something heavy was pulled across the garden towards the store. This morning, some strange pieces of burnt flesh[31] were found among the burnt wood. The police do not know if the flesh is human, but they fear the worst[P]. They are searching for Mr McFarlane. They believe that he killed Mr Oldacre and started the fire to burn his body. Inspector Lestrade of Scotland Yard is the policeman investigating the case.

'I'm surprised that you haven't been arrested already, Mr McFarlane,' said Holmes, when I had finished reading.

'I haven't been to my office this morning,' our visitor replied. 'And I haven't been to my home. It was very late when I left Mr Oldacre last night. I live in Blackheath, on the eastern edge of London, with my parents. I wasn't able to get back there, so I stayed at a hotel in Norwood. This morning, I saw the newspaper and I read about Mr Oldacre's disappearance. And I read that the police were searching for me. I decided to come straight here to consult you. I think that the police were following me when I turned into Baker Street.'

He stopped for a moment, then he added, 'Please help me, Mr Holmes. I need to protect[32] my mother from a scandal.'

At that moment there was more noise on the stairs outside and our sitting room door was thrown open. Inspector Lestrade rushed into the room. There were two more policemen behind him.

'Mr John Hector McFarlane, I arrest you for the murder of Mr Jonas Oldacre,' Lestrade said.

2

John McFarlane's Story

Holmes does not think that Lestrade is a very good detective but he is always polite to him. He has often helped Lestrade with cases which have puzzled the Scotland Yard detective.

'Lestrade, will you be kind enough[P] to let Mr McFarlane finish his story before you take him away?' Holmes asked. 'Half an hour is all we ask.'

'Well, you've helped me in the past, Mr Holmes,' the policeman replied. 'I'd like to help you now. I'll give you half an hour. But it won't help Mr McFarlane, you know. The evidence[33] against him is very strong. He'll soon be on trial[34] for murder. And you know what happens to murderers, Mr Holmes. They are executed!'

Lestrade always reminded me of a bulldog. He was short and ugly and he was always ready for a fight. But now, he sat down. He had decided to listen to the young lawyer's story.

'Yesterday afternoon, I had a visitor at my office near London Bridge Station,' McFarlane began. 'The man arrived at about three o'clock. I'd never seen him before. He told me that his name was Jonas Oldacre and that he wanted me to write his will[35] for him. He took from his pocket some pieces of paper on which he had written a draft[36] of the will. He simply wanted me to write it out again in the correct legal way.

'I read through his draft – it wasn't easy because his writing was very hard to read,' the young man went on. 'But when I'd finished reading, I was very surprised. Mr Oldacre wanted to leave all his money and everything he owned to me! Of course, I asked him why he wanted to do that. He didn't know me and I didn't know him. He told me that he knew my parents many years ago, and although he no longer saw them, he wanted to please them. He'd asked people who knew me if I was an honest man. He'd heard good things about me, and he had no family of his own, so he thought that I should have his money after his death.'

'What an interesting story,' said Holmes. 'Did you agree to write the will?'

'There was no reason for me to refuse,' McFarlane replied. 'I thought that I was a very lucky man. Mr Oldacre asked me to write the will straight away. He signed it and one of the clerks[37] in my office was the witness[38] and signed it too. He then asked me to visit him at his house in Norwood. He told me that he needed to show me some documents and he asked me to come after nine o'clock last night. He also asked me not to tell my parents about the will yet. He wanted it to be a surprise for them.'

'Have you got any proof[39] of your story, Mr McFarlane?' Holmes asked.

'The signed will is at my office, but I'll show you Mr Oldacre's draft,' McFarlane said. He took some pieces of paper from his pocket and gave them to Holmes. Holmes read them quickly and gave them to Lestrade.

'I agree with you about the writing – it is difficult to read,' Holmes told the young lawyer. 'The draft was obviously written on a train. In two places, the writing is clear. I'd guess that those parts were written in stations, when the train wasn't moving. Then there are places where the writing is worse. Those parts were written when the train *was* moving. And there are places where the writing is even worse – it's very bad indeed. Those parts were written when the train was crossing lots of points[40] which were close together.'

Then Holmes turned to the inspector. 'Well, what can we say about this draft, Lestrade?' he went on. 'It was obviously written on a train which only stopped twice during the writer's journey. And you only find lots of points close together near the main London stations. So, the draft was written on an express train[41] between Norwood and London Bridge Station, which is near this young man's office. So we can say that Mr Oldacre didn't think about his will until he was travelling to Mr McFarlane's office.'

'That's very clever, Mr Holmes,' Lestrade said. 'But it doesn't change the evidence against Mr McFarlane.'

'Well, please continue, Mr McFarlane,' said Holmes.

'When Mr Oldacre had left my office,' the young man said, 'I sent a telegram to my parents in Blackheath. I told them that I was going to meet a client and that I was going to get home very late. I didn't tell them who my client was. Then in the evening, I went to Norwood and I arrived at Mr Oldacre's house at about half-past nine.

'The old housekeeper opened the door to me,' he went on. 'Mr Oldacre greeted me and he gave me some food. Then he took me into his bedroom because he wanted to talk about some business documents. They were in his safe, which was open. We talked about the documents for a long time and I helped my client seal some of them into envelopes with wax seals. After our meeting, I couldn't find my walking stick, but Mr Oldacre said, "You'll soon be here again, my young friend. I'll find it and keep it for you." When I left the house, he was alive and well. It was nearly midnight by then. It was too late for me to get to Blackheath, so I stayed in a hotel in Norwood. This morning, I saw the newspapers and read about the disappearance. As I told you, Mr Holmes, I came straight here.'

'And now you must come with us, Mr McFarlane,' said Lestrade. 'My men will take you to Scotland Yard. I shall return to Norwood and continue my investigation. But we already know what happened, don't we? You found out that Mr Oldacre was going to leave you his money and you couldn't wait for him to die. You killed him and tried to burn his body.'

'We talked about the documents for a long time and I helped my client seal some of them into envelopes with wax seals.'

'You're wrong,' said the young man, 'and Mr Holmes will prove it!'

When McFarlane had left the house with Lestrade's two policemen, Holmes spoke to the inspector.

'I shall probably come to Norwood myself later in the day,' he said. 'But I think I shall go to Blackheath first.'

'Will you? Well, you must do what you want to do, Mr Holmes,' Lestrade said. 'But I think that you're wasting your time[P] on this case. McFarlane is guilty. It's obvious.'

He sounded sure about it, but I could tell that he wanted to know what was in Holmes's mind. And Holmes was not going to tell him!

3

Holmes Investigates

'*Will* you go to Norwood yourself, Holmes?' I asked, when Lestrade had gone.

'Yes, Watson,' he replied. 'But as I told Lestrade, I shall first go to Blackheath. This is a very strange case. Why would someone do something really important – something like drafting a will – when he was sitting on a moving train? We have to ask ourselves that question. Why wasn't Oldacre more careful about drafting his will? Is it because he didn't expect Mr McFarlane ever to get his money? It's a puzzle, isn't it?'

And soon after that, he went out.

It was evening when Holmes returned. I could see at once that he was not happy.

'Perhaps Lestrade is right after all, Watson,' he said. 'I went to Blackheath and I talked to McFarlane's mother. She told me that she'd known Jonas Oldacre long ago. "He was a terrible man and I'm pleased that he's dead," she said. She told me that Oldacre had wanted to marry her when she was a young woman. She didn't know him well, but he was a rich man and she agreed to marry him – they became engaged. But then she found out that he was wicked. She broke off the engagement[P] and told him that she never wanted to see him again. "After that, I married John's father. He was a poorer man but he was a better man," she told me. She showed me a photograph of herself which she'd given Oldacre when they were engaged. It had knife-cuts all over it. Oldacre had sent it back to her on the day she married Mr McFarlane's father. He'd told her that he'd hate her forever.

'Mrs McFarlane is quite sure that her son is not guilty of

the murder,' said Holmes. 'But she certainly hated Mr Oldacre. Perhaps her son hated him too.'

'So you think that Mr McFarlane killed Oldacre because he'd behaved badly to his mother,' I said. 'Is that the truth of the case, Holmes?'

'I'm sure that Lestrade will decide that it's the truth when he's talked to Mrs McFarlane,' Holmes replied. 'The evidence says that it might be the truth, but I can't believe it. I feel sure that someone else must have killed Oldacre. At the moment, I *can't* prove it. And Lestrade wants that young man to be executed.

'But I *have* discovered something strange,' he went on. 'I went to Norwood after I'd been to Blackheath. I saw McFarlane's walking stick with the blood on it, and the blood in the bedroom. I saw the marks which led to the timber store. It was all as the newspaper article said. But I also saw Oldacre's bank records in the house. For the last year he's been paying a large amount of money every month to someone called Mr Cornelius. I wonder who *he* is? I also talked to Oldacre's housekeeper. I'm sure that she knows more about the case than she has told the police. And I'm sure that she lied to me.'

Holmes played his violin for hours that evening. It helped him to think. He was trying to find answers to all the questions that he had about the case. But I could see that he was worried and unhappy. And he was even more worried the next morning when a telegram arrived:

> DON'T WASTE ANY MORE TIME ON THE MCFARLANE CASE. NEW EVIDENCE SHOWS THAT HE MUST BE GUILTY. LESTRADE.

'We must go to Norwood at once, Watson,' said Holmes.

When we arrived at Norwood, Lestrade was there with two other policemen. He was obviously feeling pleased with himself. 'I told you that you were wasting your time on this case, Mr Holmes,' he said. 'Now I can prove it. Come with me.'

He took us to a corridor which led from the sitting room to the kitchen. There, high on the wall, he showed us a red mark – a bloodstain[42]. It was a fingerprint[43], a very clear fingerprint.

'Well, Mr Holmes, you can't always be right,' Lestrade said. 'This time I was right and you were wrong. You know all about fingerprints and you know that every person has different fingerprints. I will prove that that is McFarlane's fingerprint.'

'I'm sure that you will,' Holmes replied calmly.

For a moment, Lestrade looked surprised. 'Well, McFarlane had Mr Oldacre's blood on his hand when he left this print,' he continued. 'The case is finished, Mr Holmes.'

'Is it? I wonder why your men didn't find the fingerprint yesterday, Lestrade,' Holmes said.

'They didn't search this corridor,' Lestrade replied. 'It didn't seem important then.'

Holmes, who had looked serious and unhappy all morning, laughed suddenly. 'It's certainly important now,' he said. 'Watson and I are going to walk in the garden for a few minutes. And then we'll look carefully at the upper floor of the house. We'll see you later, Inspector.'

When we were walking in the garden I asked why Holmes was suddenly feeling happier.

'Lestrade's men didn't search that corridor yesterday,' he told me as he paced[44] up and down. 'But I searched it. I searched it very carefully. The fingerprint wasn't there yesterday. It arrived during the night, while Mr McFarlane was in prison! I think that I understand what has happened now. Poor Lestrade will be angry.'

4

A Wicked Crime

We left the garden and we went into the house. We went upstairs, where Holmes again paced up and down. But he was still looking cheerful.

'Well it's time to finish this case, Watson,' he said after a few minutes. Holmes called down to Lestrade. 'There is some straw[45] in a shed[46] in the garden,' he told him. 'I want one of your policemen to bring some of it up here, and ask the other one to bring a bucket[47] of water up here too. And please come up yourself.'

A few moments later, the five of us were standing in the upstairs corridor. There was a pile of straw on the floor. Next to it was a bucket of water.

'What are you going to do?' Lestrade asked. He was obviously puzzled.

'Watson is going to start a small fire, Lestrade,' Holmes answered.

'Is this your idea of a joke, Mr Holmes?' the inspector said angrily.

'This is *not* a joke, Lestrade, this is very serious,' Holmes replied. 'There has been a wicked crime and a man could be executed for murder. Now, when I tell you to shout, you must all shout "Fire!" Do you understand?'

I took some matches from my pocket and lit one, then I threw the burning match into the pile of straw. A few moments later it was alight and the smell of burning straw was everywhere.

'Now!' said Holmes.

'Fire!' we all shouted.

'Again!' said Holmes.

'Fire!' we all shouted again.

'Once again!' said Holmes.

'Fire!' we all shouted once more.

At first nothing at all happened. But then, something very surprising happened. A door opened in the wall at the end of the corridor. No one could have guessed that there was a door there. It had no handle or lock on the outside and just looked like part of the wall. A moment later, a frightened old man ran out of the door towards us. He looked like a rabbit running from its hole. Holmes caught him as he tried to run past us.

'Throw the water on the straw now, Watson,' Holmes said. 'Inspector Lestrade, this is Mr Jonas Oldacre. I think that you want to talk to him. He's been hiding in the little room behind that door all the time that you've been in the house.'

The old man had an unpleasant face, grey eyes and white hair. He looked worried, but he tried to laugh. 'It was a joke,' he said. 'It was just a joke. Don't be so serious about it.'

'An innocent man was almost executed because of your joke,' Lestrade replied. He told the two policemen to take the old man downstairs. 'I'll talk to him later,' the inspector said.

'Well, Mr Holmes,' Lestrade said, when they had gone. 'You've saved the life of an innocent man. It's the best thing you've done yet! What was the clue[48] that told you that the old builder was still alive? And where did the bloodstains come from?'

'I searched the downstairs corridor yesterday,' Holmes said. 'The fingerprint wasn't there then. Someone put it there in the night. I guessed that Oldacre himself had done it. Obviously, the housekeeper was part of Oldacre's plan. She must have helped him. The small amount of blood in the bedroom is Oldacre's own blood, I think. He must have cut his finger. The housekeeper must have hidden Mr McFarlane's walking stick when he came here, so that he had to leave without it. Later, they put some blood on that too.

A moment later, a frightened old man ran out of the door towards us.

'Do you remember that Mr McFarlane told us he helped Oldacre to seal some envelopes?' Holmes went on. 'I think that the old man made sure that McFarlane pressed his finger into the hot wax. Then Oldacre made an impression of the impression with more wax, if you understand me. Last night, he used that impression and his own blood to make that fingerprint on the wall. It was a perfect copy of one of McFarlane's fingerprints. Mr Jonas Oldacre is a very clever and very wicked old man, Lestrade.'

'And how did you know about the hidden room?' Lestrade asked quietly.

'I knew that Jonas Oldacre must be hiding in the house,' Holmes replied. 'So first, I measured[49] the outside of the house. I measured it when I was pacing in the garden with Watson. Then I measured the upstairs corridor in the same way. It was shorter than it should have been, so I guessed that there was a hidden room at the end of it. It was an easy thing for a builder like Oldacre to make.'

A few minutes later we were all downstairs again. Oldacre was still trying to tell us that he had only wanted to play a joke on young Mr McFarlane.

'Oh no, it wasn't a joke, Mr Oldacre,' Holmes said to him. 'Your building firm has done badly in the last few years. You owe money to a lot of people – your creditors. You wanted to disappear and escape from them. This year, you've paid a lot of money to someone called Cornelius. I'm sure that you are really Cornelius yourself. You planned to disappear and start your life again as Mr Cornelius, in a different part of England. Your housekeeper was planning to go with you. And, of course, you've hated Mrs McFarlane for thirty years, because she refused to marry you. So you decided to take revenge[P] on her. You wanted her son to be executed. That is a serious crime, not a joke.'

'I'll take revenge on *you* for this, Sherlock Holmes,' Oldacre shouted.

'That will be difficult when you're in prison,' Holmes replied. 'I'm glad to have helped you, Lestrade,' he added, turning to the inspector. 'Come on, Watson. We must leave now.'

As we left the house, I asked Holmes about the remains in the burnt timber store – the pieces of burnt flesh.

'I expect they were rabbits, Watson,' Holmes said. 'We can never prove it. But when you write about this case, you can say that they were rabbits!'

THE SECOND STAIN

1

The Missing Document

The case which I call 'The Second Stain' was one of the most important cases of Sherlock Holmes's career. It was important for our country because it involved a diplomatic[50] secret. But it was important to us because the reputation[51] of a fine woman was in danger. We thought that Holmes needed to solve the case to save our country from a war, but in the end, we realized that in fact he had saved someone's career and someone's marriage. This is what happened.

One Tuesday morning, Holmes and I were visited in our sitting room in Baker Street by two famous men. One was Mr Trelawney Hope, the Minister[52] for European Affairs in our government. He was still quite a young man, and everyone expected great things from him in the future. He was a clever man and a handsome man, although on that morning he looked worried. Our other visitor was even more important and he looked worried too. He was our Prime Minister, the head of our government, Lord Bellinger. He was a thin, elderly man with wonderful eyes. He looked like someone who was used to having great power.

'Mr Holmes, we have a problem,' the Minister for European Affairs said. 'I have lost something, and I hope you'll be able to help me find it. As soon as I knew that it was missing – at eight o'clock this morning – I told Lord Bellinger about the problem. He suggested that you were the person that we should consult. A document has disappeared from my house, and it is extremely important that we find it quickly. Will you help us?'

'Have you told the police about this?' Holmes asked.

'No, sir, we have not told the police.' It was Lord Bellinger who answered and he spoke firmly. 'We have not told them and we *will not* tell them! Mr Holmes, if we tell the police about this, then soon the newspapers will know about it. If we tell the police, we tell the public. And it is most important that this problem remains a secret. It must *not* be made public[P].'

'And why is secrecy so important in this case?' Holmes asked.

'Because the peace of Europe may depend on it,' the Prime Minister replied seriously. 'The person who has taken the document wants to make trouble[P] for our country and for several countries in Europe. This person will try to make the contents of the document public as soon as possible.'

'I understand,' said Holmes. 'And now I will ask Mr Hope to tell us all he knows about this disappearance.'

'There is not much to tell you,' the Minister said. 'The document was a letter from the ruler of a foreign country – I must not tell you which country. The letter was received in my ministry six days ago. It was so secret that I kept it in my safe at the ministry during the daytime, and I took it home with me each evening.

'I live in Whitehall Terrace, which is close to my ministry,' he continued. 'At home, I kept the letter in my dispatch box[53], which is always locked when I am not working on its contents. The dispatch box is kept in my bedroom, which is on the second floor of my house. The letter was in the box last night. I'm sure of that because I looked at it while I was dressing for dinner.

'The box is kept on a small table beside my bed,' he went on. 'I'm a light sleeper – I wake easily if there is any noise. My wife is also a light sleeper. We're both sure that no one entered our bedroom during the night. And yet, this morning, the letter was no longer in my dispatch box.'

'At what time did you have your dinner yesterday evening? And at what time did you go to bed?' Holmes asked.

'We ate at half-past seven,' Hope replied. 'And we went to bed at half-past eleven. My wife went out to the theatre after dinner, and I read in my library until she returned.'

'So, the dispatch box was unguarded[54] for four hours,' Holmes said.

'Yes, but no one is allowed to enter our bedroom except for two servants – my wife's maid and my valet[55],' Hope said. 'They have both been with us for many years. We trust[56] them both completely. And, of course, they didn't know that there was anything especially important in the dispatch box last night.'

'Who knew about the letter?' Holmes asked.

'No one in our house knew about it,' the Minister answered. 'Even my wife knew nothing about it until this morning when I told her that it was missing.'

'How many people in Britain knew about the letter?' Holmes asked next.

'The most important members of our government knew about it,' Hope replied. 'And two or three officials who work in my ministry also knew about it. Except for those – and they are all used to keeping important secrets – no one in Britain knew. And now, it is I myself who have let this secret escape!' For a moment, the sudden despair[57] in his voice and on his face showed us his true feelings. Then he continued, more quietly again. 'And outside Britain, I'm sure that only the writer himself knew about it. I'm in regular contact with his ministers by telegram, and none of them has mentioned the letter. If they had known about it, they certainly would have contacted me.'

'Have any documents disappeared from your house before this?' Holmes asked.

'No, never,' Hope replied. 'Never.'

2

The Contents of the Letter

The room was silent for several minutes as Holmes thought about the problem. At last he spoke.

'I now need to know more about this letter,' he said. 'What was in it? Why has its disappearance worried you so much? Why is getting it back so important?'

It was the Prime Minister who answered. 'All I can tell you, Mr Holmes, is that the letter is in a long, thin, pale-blue envelope,' he said. 'There is a large, red, wax seal on the envelope and it is addressed to Mr Trelawney Hope. I cannot tell you anything about the contents of the letter. Please use your famous powers of deduction[58], and if you can find an envelope which matches this description, you will have done a great thing for your country. You do not need to know what the letter says, and I cannot tell you. That is a diplomatic secret which I cannot share with you.'

Holmes stood up and smiled at our visitors. 'You are two of the busiest men in the country,' he said, 'and I am busy too. I cannot help you with this problem, and I shall waste your time and my own time if we talk any more. I'm sorry.'

Lord Bellinger got up quickly. It was obvious that he was used to having his own way[P]. 'Mr Holmes –' he began angrily. For a moment, I thought that there was going to be an unpleasant disagreement. Then he continued, more quietly, 'Well, we must accept your request to know what the letter is about. Please sit down again and listen to me.'

'You can trust us with your secret,' Holmes said. 'We are men of honour[P].'

'I told you earlier that the letter was written by the ruler of a foreign country,' the Prime Minister said. 'Recently this ruler has been worried by our policy[59] in parts of our empire[60]. His worry was unnecessary – our policy is not a danger to him or his country. But he suddenly became very angry about our policy and he wrote the letter to our government in anger. He did not consult his own ministers about it. Even now, they know nothing about his action. And now, the ruler himself is calmer. He understands that writing the letter was not a good idea. I believe that he wants us to pretend[61] that it never existed. That is why no one else must ever see it.'

Holmes held up his hand and Lord Bellinger paused. Holmes wrote something on a small piece of paper and passed it to him.

'Yes, Mr Holmes,' the Prime Minister said. 'You are right. That is the name of the ruler I am talking about. His letter contained shocking[62] accusations[63] about this country. If it is made public, there will be great anger here against his country. We will soon be at war with them. It will cost us millions of pounds and it will cost us thousands of men – young men who will be killed.'

'So this ruler doesn't want the letter to be made public, and our government doesn't want it to be made public,' Holmes said. 'Who *does* want the letter to be made public?'

'There are two alliances – groups of countries – in Europe who are fierce rivals[64], Mr Holmes,' Lord Bellinger replied. 'I'm sure you know that. If Britain is at war with one of them, that will be greatly to the advantage of[P] the other. Do you understand me?'

Trelawney Hope, who had been quiet, groaned[65] in despair at these words. The Prime Minister put his hand on the younger man's shoulder. 'It is not your fault,' he said kindly. 'You acted with honour and you acted with care.'

Perhaps this was true, but Trelawney Hope's career would be ruined[66] if we could not recover the letter. The news that he had lost the document would create a scandal.

'The facts are simple, then,' Holmes said. 'If we cannot get this document back soon, there will be a European war.'

'That's the truth, Mr Holmes,' Lord Bellinger replied. 'What will you do? The government will pay you any amount of money that you need. And what do you advise me to do?'

'It is obvious that someone in the Minister's household took the letter,' Holmes replied. Trelawney Hope started to say again that he trusted his servants completely, but Holmes stopped him.

'Your bedroom is on the second floor of your house,' Holmes went on. 'No one could get into the *room* directly from outside the house. No stranger could get into the *house* without being seen by a member of your household. So, someone in the house took the letter. He or she must have given it to one of the international spies who live and work in London. I can think of only three spies who might have it. I will begin by finding out if any of them has left the country suddenly, last night or this morning. The person who has it won't post it. They'll take it personally to where it can cause the most trouble. It is probably too late for us to get the letter back. I will do my best for you[P], but I must advise you, Lord Bellinger, to get ready for war.'

3

A Visit from a Lady

When our visitors had left, Holmes was silent for a long time. He sat in his chair, thinking about our new problem, as I read the morning newspaper. There had been a shocking crime – a murder – in London the previous evening and the paper had a story about it.

At last, Holmes looked up. He was ready to talk again.

'Perhaps we are not too late after all, Watson,' he began. 'Perhaps we still have some hope. I must find out which of those three spies had the letter. Perhaps he still has it. Perhaps he is waiting to see who offers him the most money for it. It's possible that I could buy it back. Our government will pay any price.'

'But who *are* the three spies you mentioned?' I asked. 'How do you know that one of them has the letter?'

'There are only three spies who live in London and who could have done this, Watson,' said Holmes. 'Oberstein, La Rothiere and Eduardo Lucas. I must try to talk to all three of them.'

'Does Eduardo Lucas live in Godolphin Street, Holmes?' I asked.

'Yes, that's the man,' Holmes replied. He was surprised that I knew.

'Then I'm afraid you won't see him,' I said. I opened the newspaper and pointed to a story. 'He was murdered last night at his house.'

Holmes was obviously shocked by my news. He took the newspaper from me and read the story.

A mysterious crime was committed in London last night. It happened in a beautiful house in Godolphin

Street, near the Parliament buildings in Westminster. The owner of the house, Mr Eduardo Lucas, was found dead with a knife in his body. Mr Lucas was aged thirty-four and was not married. Mr Lucas lived in the house with an elderly housekeeper, Mrs Pringle, and a valet, John Mitton. Last night, Mrs Pringle was in her room at the top of the house and Mitton was not at home. At a quarter to twelve, a policeman saw that the front door was open. He knocked on the door to ask if anything was wrong. There was no reply, but he saw that there was a light on in the front room. He entered the room and found Mr Lucas lying dead on the floor.

The knife, which was still in Mr Lucas's body, was his own property. It had hung on a wall in the room for some years. Much of the furniture in the room had been turned over. But the strange thing is that nothing in the room had been stolen. It seems that burglary[67] was not the reason for the crime. Inspector Lestrade of Scotland Yard is in charge of the case for the police.

'Well, Watson,' said Holmes when he had finished reading. 'What do you think about this?'

'It's an amazing coincidence[68], Holmes,' I replied.

'I don't believe it. It can't be a coincidence,' said Holmes. 'There must be a connection between this crime and the one we are trying to solve.'

'Is the missing letter still our problem?' I asked. 'The police must know everything now.'

'No, Watson, you're wrong. They won't know about the letter,' Holmes said. 'The Prime Minister still won't tell them about that. We are the only people who know about both crimes, and we are the only people who can find the connection between them. The first thing that seems interesting is that Godolphin Street is very close to Whitehall Terrace. That's a kind of connection between the households – Lucas's and Hope's. The other two spies live much further to the west. If Lucas had the letter, he probably had an accomplice[69] in Hope's household. Now we must look for more connections.'

Shortly after that, Holmes's thinking was interrupted by a surprising visitor. It was Lady[70] Hilda Hope. Lady Hilda, we knew, was the wife of Mr Trelawney Hope, who had already visited us that morning.

The lady who entered the room was one of the most beautiful young women in London. But that day, she looked pale and very frightened.

'Mr Holmes,' she said, 'I think that my husband has already been here today. Before I say anything else, I must ask you to keep my visit a secret. My husband must never know about it. Please promise me that.'

'I cannot promise anything until I know the reason for your visit,' Holmes replied. 'Please sit down and tell us why you have come.'

'I will tell you the truth, Mr Holmes,' Lady Hilda said. 'I hope that, in return, you will tell me the truth. My husband and I have no secrets from each other, except in one area of life – the area of politics. He refuses to talk about politics with me. Now, I understand that something terrible happened in our house last night. I understand that a document has disappeared, and that its loss is very serious. I know that my husband consulted you about this loss this morning. Will you tell me what the document is, Mr Holmes? My husband is in despair and I want to help him, but he won't tell me what the problem is. If *you* can tell me what has really happened, I will do my best to help him.'

'Lady Hilda,' Holmes replied, 'I cannot tell you and I cannot help you. I promised complete secrecy to your husband and to Lord Bellinger. If your husband won't tell you what has disappeared, it's not in my power to tell you. I'm sorry.'

'If you won't tell me that, Mr Holmes, will you answer this question?' Lady Hilda asked. 'Will this disappearance be bad for my husband's political career? Will it ruin his reputation?'

'Yes,' said Holmes, 'it will be bad for his career. I think I can tell you that.'

'And is our country in danger as a result of this disappearance?' Lady Hilda went on.

'Yes, it is,' Holmes answered. 'But I cannot tell you any more.'

'Then I hope you will do as I asked and keep my visit a secret,' said Lady Hilda. Then she turned and left the room.

After we heard the front door close behind her, Holmes laughed. 'I wonder what she really wanted,' he said. 'Well, Watson, I'm going out. I'm going to Godolphin Street to see what the police are doing about Eduardo Lucas's murder. Our friend Inspector Lestrade will tell me all about it. And I might be able to help him. I'll see you later in the day.'

'Holmes,' I said, as he put on his coat. 'What is your theory? What connects the two crimes?'

'We must never make theories before we have facts, Watson,' he replied.

4

Information from France

During the next three days, I did not see Holmes often. He went out and came in at strange hours. He sometimes stopped to eat a sandwich and sometimes he played his violin for a few minutes. This always helped him to think, he said. But he told me little. I learnt more from the newspapers than I did from Holmes.

There was an inquest[71] into Eduardo Lucas's death. The jury[72] decided that he had been murdered. But that was obvious, and they could not say who the killer was, of course. One day, Inspector Lestrade arrested John Mitton, the dead man's valet. Lestrade had found a few things that had belonged to Lucas in Mitton's room. He decided that Lucas had discovered that Mitton was a thief and that Mitton had killed Lucas to avoid prosecution[73]. But the valet explained that the things had been gifts from his employer. The housekeeper knew about these gifts and agreed with Mitton's explanation. And the man's alibi for the night of the murder was strong – he had visited friends on the other side of London. The police interviewed his friends and soon Lestrade had to release[74] Mitton.

'Watson,' said Holmes on the third day, 'I'm sorry. I haven't told you anything about our case. But that's because there's nothing to tell you. Lestrade has discovered nothing and I haven't done any better.

'The police are sure that it wasn't a burglar who killed Lucas,' Holmes went on. 'No valuable objects were taken. The police have now read all the papers in the dead man's desk, but that hasn't helped them. The papers prove that Lucas was friendly with many politicians in several different countries and that he was able to speak many languages. They prove that he wrote and received a huge number of letters. But to Lestrade, there's nothing suspicious[75] about any of this. He doesn't know that Lucas was a spy and I'm not going to tell him. We must keep our secret.'

The police had discovered something though. They learnt that Lucas spent a lot of time in Paris each year. He sometimes stayed there for several months at a time.

'The only strange thing is that he never took his valet to France with him,' said Holmes. 'Mitton always stayed in London when Lucas was away from home. But that fact doesn't really help us to solve the mystery of his death.'

Then, on the fourth day, everything changed. One of the newspapers published a story about a long telegram which the London police had received from Paris. I showed the story to Holmes as he ate his breakfast.

> Our readers know about the mysterious death of Mr Eduardo Lucas at his house in Westminster. Earlier this week, the police arrested and then released the dead man's valet. Now we can tell our readers that Mr Lucas has for many years had a double life. Yesterday, the servants of a woman in Paris reported to the French police that she had become mentally ill and was behaving dangerously. The woman, Madame Fournaye, was taken immediately to a hospital. Last Tuesday, she had returned from a short trip to London in a desperate state. She had also lost her memory.
>
> Her servants told the police that a man sometimes lived with her at her house in Paris. He used the name of Henri Fournaye, and the servants believed that he was her husband. But photographs have proved that this man was the same man who was known in London as Eduardo Lucas. Madame Fournaye's servants also told the police that she has always been an angry and jealous person. It seems that

> she travelled to London on Monday. Perhaps she went to confront[76] Mr Lucas about his double life. Perhaps she killed him because she was jealous. Perhaps she then lost her memory because of the shock of her crime, or perhaps she was already mentally ill when she killed the man.
>
> A photograph of this woman has been shown to people who live near Mr Lucas's house in Westminster. Several of them have told the police that a woman who looked like Madame Fournaye was in Godolphin Street on Monday. She was there for several hours and she seemed to be watching Mr Lucas's house. The French doctors do not believe that she will ever recover her memory. They believe she will have to remain in hospital for the rest of her life. She will not be prosecuted for the murder of Eduardo Lucas.

'Well, this doesn't help us much,' Holmes said when he had finished reading.

'But Holmes, it explains Lucas's death,' I said.

'Ah, Watson, the man's death is not important,' Holmes replied. 'It's just a detail. Our job is to save Europe from war, not to discover who killed Eduardo Lucas. Only one important thing has happened in the last few days and that is that nothing has happened.'

'What do you mean, Holmes?' I asked.

'Well, I get news from the government almost every hour,' Holmes replied. 'If there were any signs of trouble beginning in any European country, I'd know about it. And there are no signs of that happening. So the letter hasn't reached anyone who could make trouble by publishing it. But we still need to know who has it.'

At that moment, a boy entered the room with a telegram for Holmes.

'It's from Lestrade, Watson,' Holmes said when he had read it. 'He wants me to go to Godolphin Street. Perhaps he needs our help.'

5

At Godolphin Street

We soon arrived at Lucas's house in Godolphin Street. It was my first visit to the scene of the crime. There was a big policeman standing outside the front door. He let us into the house, and in the front room we found Inspector Lestrade. As usual, I thought he looked like a bulldog. The only sign of the crime in the room was a large bloodstain on the beautiful square carpet. This carpet covered only the centre part of the floor, which was made from small wooden blocks[77]. The wood had been polished and was quite shiny.

'Have you seen the news from Paris?' Lestrade asked Holmes. 'That poor woman is obviously the killer. There's no doubt about it.'

'If you're sure about it, why do you need my help?' Holmes replied.

'Well, I don't really need your *help*, Mr Holmes,' said Lestrade. 'But I want to show you something. After we had received the news from Paris about Madame Fournaye, we were tidying the room this morning because our work is finished here. That's when we discovered something strange. It's a kind of puzzle and I know how much you like puzzles, Mr Holmes. Do you see the stain on the carpet? Lucas's blood has soaked through it. Now look at this!'

He pulled back the corner of the carpet nearest the large bloodstain and pointed at the wooden floor that the carpet had covered. There was no bloodstain on the wood. There was certainly blood on the underside of the carpet, and there should have been a stain on the wood it had covered. But there was no stain on the wood. Then Lestrade lifted another part of the carpet which had *no* bloodstain on it, and he showed us a large stain on the wooden floor beneath it. Holmes looked surprised and Lestrade laughed.

'Here's the second stain,' he said. 'What do you make of that?[P]'

'Well, someone must have turned the carpet round,' said Holmes.

'Yes,' Lestrade agreed, 'that's obvious. We Scotland Yard men don't need the famous detective, Mr Sherlock Holmes, to tell us that. But why, Mr Holmes? *Why* has someone moved it, and who was it?'

Holmes thought for a minute. I could see from his face that he had suddenly had an idea and was excited about it.

'Has the policeman at the front door been here all the time since the body was discovered, Lestrade?' he asked.

'Yes, Mr Holmes,' the inspector replied. 'Constable MacPherson has been here all week.'

'Well, this is my advice,' Holmes said. 'Interview him immediately. Ask him why he let a stranger into this room. Don't ask him *if* he let someone in. Tell him that you *know* he did, but you want to know *why*. Tell him he can save his career if he tells the truth. Get the whole story from him. And, Lestrade – take him to the back of the house when you interview him. He won't tell you the truth if he thinks that we will hear it too.'

As soon as Lestrade had gone, Holmes pulled the carpet to one side and got down onto the floor. He started to examine[78] the wooden blocks carefully.

'We don't have much time, Watson,' he said. 'There must be a hiding place somewhere under the floor.' He searched quickly and, two minutes later, he said, 'Ah, here it is!'

He pulled at the edge of one of the wooden blocks and carefully lifted it out. Holmes put his hand into the opening and searched it. But when he took his hand out again, it was empty.

Holmes put his hand into the opening and searched it.

'It's gone!' he said angrily. 'It was here, I'm sure of that, but now it's gone. Be quick and help me put the carpet back in its place. We mustn't tell Lestrade about this.'

We had just replaced the carpet when Lestrade came back into the room. He was followed by the policeman, whose face was red.

'You were right, Mr Holmes,' Lestrade said. 'This foolish[79] man did let a stranger in here. Tell them about it, MacPherson.'

'It was a young lady, sir,' the policeman said. 'She came to the door yesterday evening. She said that she thought she knew someone who lived here, but that she must have got the address wrong. But when I told her that there had been a crime here, she said that she had read about it in the newspaper. She asked if she could just look into the room where it had happened. She was very curious about it. Well, sir, I get lonely here on my own and she was a very pretty young lady. I didn't think that it would cause any trouble if I let her look into the room. So she came in, but when she saw the bloodstain on the carpet, she fainted and fell onto the floor.

'I got some water for her, but she didn't recover. So I ran to the public house[80] at the corner of the street and bought some brandy[81] for her. When I got back, she had gone. I'm sorry if what I did was wrong, sir.'

'So, the woman was alone while you went to the public house?' Holmes asked.

'That's right, sir,' MacPherson replied.

'Did you move the carpet last night?' Holmes asked. 'Think carefully.'

'Well, sir, when the young lady fainted, she fell on the carpet and it moved across the polished floor,' MacPherson said. 'It was very twisted[82] so I moved it back and straightened it. I tried to make it look tidy.'

'And you say that your visitor was a very pretty young lady?' Holmes asked.

'She was beautiful, sir,' MacPherson said. 'She was beautiful.'

'Well, we must go now, Watson,' Holmes said suddenly. 'There's nothing we can do here and we have an important visit to make.'

Lestrade stayed in the room when we left, but the policeman came to the door with us. As we were leaving, Holmes took something out of his pocket and showed it to the man.

'Good heavens[P], sir!' the policeman said. 'You must be a magician!'

And Holmes started to laugh.

6

At Whitehall Terrace

'Where are we going, Holmes?' I asked as we walked away from the house.

'We're going to Whitehall Terrace, Watson, to see the last act of this strange play,' he replied.

When we arrived at Mr Trelawney Hope's house, Holmes asked to see Lady Hilda. We were shown into a large sitting room, and a minute later Lady Hilda Hope entered. She looked pale and frightened.

'Mr Holmes,' she said, 'you are unkind. You should not have come here. I do not want my husband to know about my visit to you – I told you that. He must not find out that I have talked to you. He will be home very soon. I must ask you to leave immediately.'

'Lady Hilda, I have been asked by your husband to recover a document,' Holmes replied. 'I am sorry, but the only way I could do that was to come here. Where is the letter, Lady Hilda? I know that you know where it is. Please tell me the truth, and I will help you.'

'You are very wrong, Mr Holmes, and you have insulted[83] me,' the young woman said angrily. 'Get out of my house. I shall ring the bell for the butler[84] and ask him to make you leave.' She looked desperate, but it was obvious that she was not going to admit that Holmes was right. She began walking towards the bell.

'If you do that, we will not be able to save your husband from a scandal,' said Holmes. 'His reputation and his career will be ruined. Your life will be ruined. I ask you again, Lady Hilda, please tell me the truth.'

'I can tell you nothing!' she said.

'Then I will tell you what *I* know,' Holmes replied. 'I know that you visited Eduardo Lucas on Monday evening and gave him the missing document. I know that you returned to his house last night. I know that you found the hiding place under the carpet. I know that you recovered the document from it. I know that because I showed this picture to the policeman at the house. He recognized it immediately.'

He took from his pocket a small picture which he had cut from a magazine. It was a portrait of Lady Hilda Hope.

'Lady Hilda,' Holmes went on, 'I do not wish to cause any trouble for you. When I have recovered the letter, my job here is finished. I will not share your secret with anyone. I will not tell your husband about it. But I must have the letter.'

'You are obviously unwell, Mr Holmes,' the woman said. 'You are mad. You are talking nonsense. Leave this house now.'

Then Holmes surprised her. He rang the bell for the butler himself. When the man appeared, Holmes asked to see Mr Trelawney Hope. 'I have something very important to tell him,' he said coldly.

'Mr Hope is not here now, but he will return in fifteen minutes,' the butler said. 'He is bringing the Prime Minister home for luncheon[85].'

'I will wait for him,' Holmes replied.

As soon as the butler left the room, Lady Hilda started to cry. She had tried to fight us but she could not go on fighting. She knelt in front of Holmes and looked up at him. The tears ran down her beautiful face.

'I will tell you the truth,' she said. 'I see now that I *must* tell you. But please don't tell my husband what I am going to say to you. It would break his heart.'

Holmes helped her to stand up. 'I'm glad that you have decided to do the right thing,' he said. 'I will do everything I can to help you. But we don't have much time. Your husband will soon be here. Where is the letter?'

Lady Hilda ran to a writing desk in the corner of the room, unlocked it with a key, and took out a long, thin, blue envelope.

'Here it is,' she said, bitterly. 'I wish I had never seen it!'

'How can we return it to your husband without him knowing that you had it, I wonder?' Holmes said. 'Where is your husband's dispatch box?'

'It's still in our bedroom,' Lady Hilda replied.

'Please go and get it quickly,' said Holmes.

Lady Hilda quickly returned with the box.

'How did you open it when you took the letter?' Holmes asked her. Then he answered his own question. 'Of course, you copied the key,' he said, before she could speak. 'Open the box, please.'

Lady Hilda took a small key from a pocket in her dress and opened the dispatch box. It was full of documents. Holmes pushed the letter between the pages of one of the thick documents near the bottom of the box. In a few minutes, the box was back in its place in the bedroom.

7

Diplomatic Secrets

When Lady Hilda returned to the sitting room, Holmes smiled.

'We have done our best to protect your reputation,' he said. 'We now have ten minutes before your husband returns. Will you tell me why you took the letter?'

'I will tell you the whole story,' Lady Hilda said. 'When I said that I kept no secrets from my husband, I wasn't telling you the truth. Many years ago, when I was an innocent girl, I wrote a letter to someone – a man. This was before I knew my husband. It was a foolish letter, but it was the letter of a young girl in love for the first time. I did not understand that it could cause trouble for me in the future. Until recently, I thought that the whole thing was forgotten long ago. Then, last week, I heard from Mr Eduardo Lucas. He told me that he had my letter. He also told me that my husband had a document which he wanted. One of the officials in my husband's ministry had sold him the information. Lucas said that I must steal the document for him. He said that if I did not steal it, he would send my letter to my husband.

'I knew that if my husband saw my letter, he would lose his trust in me,' she went on. 'He has a very strong sense of honour and he would not understand that I wrote the letter innocently. I didn't know what was in the document that Lucas wanted. Please believe that. Lucas didn't tell me and my husband has never talked to me about his work. I thought that my happiness and my marriage were much more important than any political document could be. I didn't know that the document was so important to the peace of Europe, Mr Holmes. I only learnt that when I spoke to you, after I had taken it.

'I made a wax impression of my husband's key,' Lady Hilda said. 'Lucas made a new key from the impression and gave it to me. On Monday evening I used the new key to steal the document, then I went out. I told my husband I was going to the theatre, but I took the document to Lucas's house. In the street outside the house, I noticed a woman. I knocked on the door and Lucas let me in. He didn't close the door because I only meant to stay a moment. We went into the front room and we made the exchange – Lucas gave me my letter and I gave him the document.

'Suddenly, there was a noise in the hall outside the room,' she continued. 'Lucas quickly pulled back a corner of the carpet and hid the document in a hole under the floor. He had just replaced the carpet when a woman entered the room – the woman I had seen outside the house. She screamed at Lucas. She said that she had caught him with his other wife at last. She took a knife that was hanging on the wall and she attacked him.

'There was a struggle, and the furniture was turned over,' Lady Hilda said. 'But the woman was strong and she stabbed Lucas with the knife. I ran from the house as fast as I could. You know the rest of the story, Mr Holmes. Last night, I recovered the document. But I couldn't think of a way of giving it back to my husband without telling him the truth. And I couldn't do that. It would have been the end of our marriage.'

As she finished speaking, we heard the front door open. A moment later, Trelawney Hope and Lord Bellinger entered the room.

'Have you got good news for us, Mr Holmes?' Hope asked.

'Yes, I no longer believe that this country is in danger,' said Holmes.

'That is certainly good news,' said Hope. Then he spoke to his wife. 'Will you leave us for a few minutes, my dear? We need to talk about politics. We will join you soon for lunch.'

When Lady Hilda had left the room, Holmes spoke to Trelawney Hope.

'Mr Hope,' he said, 'I believe that you have made a mistake. I don't believe that the missing letter ever left this house. If it had, someone would have published it by now. I don't believe that it ever left your dispatch box. I think it has probably become mixed up with the other papers in the box. Will you search the box again, please?'

Trelawney Hope started to argue with Holmes. 'This is not the time to joke. I'm quite sure that the letter is *not* in the dispatch box,' he said angrily.

But then Lord Bellinger spoke. 'We can easily decide who is right,' he said. 'Send for the box, Hope, and we will search it here.'

Hope walked to the bell and rang for his valet. He told the man to bring the dispatch box from his bedroom. When the valet returned to the room with it, the Minister for European Affairs took a small key from his pocket and opened the box. He started to search through the papers.

'As you can see, Mr Holmes,' he began, 'the letter is not–' Then he stopped. 'Good heavens!' he said. He held up the thin, blue envelope. 'You were right, it *was* here. And I'm very happy to see it. You must be a magician, Mr Holmes. How did you know it was in the box, after all?'

'I knew it was there because I knew that it was nowhere else,' Holmes replied with a smile.

'I must go and tell my wife,' said the Minister. 'She will be as happy as I am. She has been so worried about the disappearance.' He quickly left the room.

Lord Bellinger looked carefully at Holmes's face. His wonderful eyes were smiling brightly.

'How did the letter really get back into the box, Mr Holmes?' he asked quietly.

'Ah. *We* also have our diplomatic secrets!' Holmes replied.

THE STOCKBROKER'S[86] CLERK

1

Hall Pycroft's Story

One Saturday morning, several months after I got married, Sherlock Holmes called at my house. At that time I was working as a doctor again, and I did not often see my old friend. But I was always pleased when I saw him. And I was pleased to hear his voice in my hall when my servant let him in on that fine June morning.

'Are you busy today, Watson?' he asked, as he entered my consulting room. 'Could you travel to Birmingham with me today? A young man came to consult me this morning about a very interesting problem. I'm going to investigate it. It's the kind of case that always used to interest you, and I thought that you'd like to help me.'

'Yes, I'll certainly come with you,' I replied. 'I'm not busy today. I'll just go and tell my wife that I'm going out.'

'That's excellent, Watson,' said Holmes. 'I won't tell you about the case myself. The young man who consulted me is waiting in a cab outside your door. He'll tell you his own story when we join him.'

Five minutes later, we had begun our journey.

The man in the cab was a pleasant-looking young Londoner called Hall Pycroft. He had an honest face, fair hair and a little yellow moustache. He wore a black suit and looked like many of the young men who worked in London's financial district. And that is what he did too – he was a stockbroker's clerk. He didn't say much as the cab took us to Euston Station. He waited until we were on the train to Birmingham before he told me about his problem.

'I feel like a fool now, Dr Watson,' he began. 'I'm sure that I've been cheated[87], and I still don't quite know why. But I'll tell you the whole story.

'Until recently I worked for a firm of stockbrokers called Coxon and Woodhouse. It was a good firm and I did well there for five years. But two months ago, the firm crashed. It lost a lot of money on the stock market and all the clerks like me lost their jobs. So there were twenty-seven of us who were suddenly out of work. We were all trying to get new jobs at the same time. We read all the job advertisements in the newspapers. But unfortunately, there weren't many advertisements for stockbrokers' clerks.

'I'd saved some money,' the young man went on. 'I lived on that and wrote to every firm of London stockbrokers that advertised a job. But for more than a month I had no luck. I'd spent almost all of my money when I saw an advertisement for a clerk's job at Mawson and Williams. Mawson's is one of the biggest, richest firms in London. They deal in[88] very valuable securities[89]. If you wanted to apply for the job, you had to write a letter to the manager – you weren't interviewed in person. Well, some days after I sent my letter, I received a reply from Mawson's. My luck had changed. The reply said that I'd got the job and that I must arrive for work there the following Monday. That was *last* Monday, in fact.

'I was very pleased with the news and I was looking forward to starting work for such a good firm,' Mr Pycroft said. 'But that same evening I had a visitor. I live in a room in a house in north London and the man came to see me there. He said that his name was Arthur Pinner.'

'Will you describe this man for Dr Watson, please?' Holmes asked.

'Yes, of course. Well, he wasn't very tall,' Mr Pycroft replied. 'He had dark eyes and black hair and he had a black beard too. He seemed honest.

'My visitor knew that I had been looking for a job,' the young man continued. 'And he knew that I now had one at Mawson's. He said that he'd heard about me from people in the financial district. He told me that everyone had said that I was clever and good at my job. He said that Mr Parker, my manager at Coxon's, had said that I would do well in *any* job. Mr Pinner asked me if I'd still read about the financial markets while I was out of work. When I said that I had, he tested me. He asked me to tell him that day's prices for the shares of several different companies. I read the financial newspapers every day and I remember things easily, so I knew the answers to his questions.

'Mr Pinner was pleased with my answers, and he said that he had an offer for me,' the young man told me. 'He offered me another job – "It's a much better job," he said.'

2

A Better Offer

As we continued on our journey towards Birmingham, Mr Pycroft went on with his story.

'My visitor told me that he had a brother, whose name was Harry Pinner. This brother had recently become the managing director of a large company, he said. And he had asked *my* Mr Pinner to find a man who could be the business manager for that company.'

'And what was the name of this company?' I asked.

'It was called the Franco-Midland Hardware Company,' said the young man. 'I'd never heard of it, Dr Watson, and I told Mr Pinner that. He replied that it wasn't well known in Britain. But he said that it *was* well known in France, where it had 134 shops. These shops sold things like knives, glasses, cups, plates and household equipment. The hardware was all made in Britain, in the Midlands – the area around Birmingham – but it was sold only in France. The company was still growing and it was going to have a great future, Mr Pinner said.

'Well, I told him that I'd had a hard fight to get a job after Coxon's had crashed,' Mr Pycroft went on. 'I said that I didn't want to throw away my new job with Mawson's. And I said that I knew nothing about hardware, so I didn't understand why he wanted me for the job. Mr Pinner replied, "Ah, but you know about *figures*! That's the important thing!" He told me that I could earn five hundred pounds a year at his brother's company. He took a hundred pounds from his pocket and put it on my table. He said that I could have it immediately as part of my first year's pay, if I took the job.'

The young man paused for a moment, then he continued his story.

'Obviously, I wanted to know more about the job,' he said. 'First of all, I wanted to know where I would be working. Mr Pinner told me, "You'll need to talk to my brother about that. His office is in Birmingham. But I think that you'll have to move to Paris. That's where the company's main office is." Well, his offer sounded very exciting. In my new job at Mawson's I was only going to earn two hundred pounds a year. Now I was being offered five hundred. In the end, I accepted his offer. I told Mr Pinner that I would take the job with the Franco-Midland Hardware Company.

'Mr Pinner asked me to write a letter to him straight away, while he sat in my room,' Hall Pycroft said. 'I had to write that I agreed to take the job at the Franco-Midland Hardware Company. I thought that was strange, Dr Watson, because I had already told him that I wanted the job. You don't usually have to write a letter when you accept that kind of job – word of mouth[90] is enough. As I wrote the letter, he wrote a letter to his brother, telling him that I was now the company's business manager. He took my letter and gave me the one he had written. He told me to go to the company's office at 126 Corporation Street in Birmingham at one o'clock the next day. His brother would meet me there, he said, and would read the letter he had just given me. "It's only a temporary office," he said. "My brother is still looking for a better one." Well, that was all right. I was free the next day and I could take the train to Birmingham, I told him.

'Mr Pinner was very pleased. He then asked me what I was going to do about Mawson's,' the young man continued. 'I said that I would write to them immediately and refuse their job. But Mr Pinner said, "No, don't do that." I asked him why, and he told me that he had made a bet[91] with Mawson's manager. He'd already told me that he had talked to Mr Parker – my manager at Coxon's – about me. But now he said that he'd also visited the manager at Mawson's to ask about me.

'Mr Pinner told me that the Mawson's manager had become angry with him,' Hall Pycroft continued. 'He thought that Mr Pinner was trying to steal his clerks. Mr Pinner said he told the manager that if he wanted good people, he should pay them well. But the manager had laughed and said he was sure that I wouldn't listen to his offer. He said he knew me well and that he had saved me from poverty[92] by offering me a job. He said I would happily work for him for less money than Mr Pinner was offering. They had had an argument about me. Mr Pinner told me, "I said that you wouldn't arrive for work on Monday. In fact, I said that he would never hear from you again. I bet him five pounds that I was right and it would please me to win that bet!" Well, that's what Mr Pinner told me and I believed his story. I had no reason not to believe it.'

'We understand that,' Holmes said. 'Please continue.'

'Mr Pinner's story made me angry,' Mr Pycroft went on. 'I told him that I'd never met the manager at Mawson's and that he knew nothing about me at all. He had obviously pretended to know me so that Mr Pinner would not talk to me about the job. I decided that I owed Mawson's nothing. I agreed that I wouldn't write to them, and Mr Pinner would win his five pounds. He laughed when I told him that. Then he stood up, gave me the hundred pounds and left my room.'

3

The Dusty Office

'This is all very interesting, isn't it, Watson?' Holmes said. 'The letter which this Mr Pinner asked our friend to write interests me the most. Please go on, Mr Pycroft.'

'Well, the next morning – it was last Saturday, Dr Watson – I took the train to Birmingham,' Mr Pycroft went on. 'I found a room in a hotel, and then I walked to Corporation Street. I arrived a little early and found number 126, which was a large building containing many offices. The names of lots of different firms were painted on a board by the front door. Each name had a floor number and a room number. I looked for the Franco-Midland Hardware Company's name but I couldn't find it. I was wondering what to do when a man came towards me. He looked very like the man who had visited me the previous evening, but the colour of his hair was lighter and he was clean shaven – he didn't have a beard. I guessed that he must be my visitor's brother.

'The man spoke first,' our young friend said. 'He said, "You must be Mr Hall Pycroft. I'm Harry Pinner. My brother sent me a telegram to say that you were coming." He said that he was pleased that I wanted the job.

'I told him I'd been trying to find his office. "It isn't on the board," I said. He laughed. "Well, it's only a temporary office," he replied. "We won't be here for long. Please follow me." He turned towards the stairs.

'So I followed Mr Harry Pinner up many stairs, to the top floor of the building, and along a corridor,' Mr Pycroft told me. 'At the end of the corridor there were two rooms with a door between them. The rooms weren't very big and they were very dusty. I thought that they hadn't been used for a long time. There was an old table and one chair in the first room. The door to the second room was open, and I saw only a chair in there. I started to worry about my decision. I had been expecting to see large offices with new furniture and lots of clerks working at desks. My surprise must have been written on my face[P], because Mr Pinner said, "Rome wasn't built in a day[P], my boy. Don't worry, the Franco-Midland has lots of money." I remembered the hundred pounds in my pocket and I felt better.

'Mr Pinner took the letter from his brother that I had brought with me,' the young man went on. 'He read it quickly and said, "My brother thinks you are a very clever young man. I hope that you will enjoy working for us." He told me that after a week I would be sent to Paris, but for the next few days I must stay in Birmingham. There were several tasks for me to do there.

'He showed me the first task immediately,' said Mr Pycroft. 'A large red book lay on the dusty desk. "This is a list of the names and addresses of all the people in Paris," he told me. "After each name is a note of what work they do, or what firms they own. I want you to draw a line under the names and addresses of all the people and firms that sell china and glass. Perhaps they will buy the stock for their firms from us if we talk to them." He told me to take the book back to my hotel and do the task there. "Bring the work to me here on Monday, at twelve o'clock," he said.

'I was surprised. I thought that there were already lists which gave that kind of information,' Mr Pycroft continued. 'I thought that the task was unnecessary and I told Mr Pinner that, but he said that the lists weren't up to date. He needed the latest information, he said. Well, I worked for the rest of the day, and I worked on Sunday and on Monday morning too. But I was only halfway through the task. I took the book to Mr Pinner in the dusty office, and told him I had not finished the

'I want you to draw a line under the names and addresses of all the people and firms that sell china and glass.'

task. He told me not to worry about it. I had to continue with the task and visit him again on Wednesday. On that day, the work was still unfinished and he told me to see him again on Friday – that was yesterday.

'Yesterday, I took the finished task to Mr Pinner,' the young man said. 'He thanked me, and told me that my next task was to make a list of all the furniture shops. "They sell glass and china too," he said. He told me to visit him again this evening at seven o'clock. "Don't work too hard," he said. "A young man needs to have some fun, don't you agree?" He laughed when he said this and I noticed something that shocked me. When he laughed, I saw that one of Harry Pinner's teeth, on the left-hand side of his mouth, had a gold filling. The work had been done very badly.

'What shocked me, Dr Watson,' the young man said, 'was this: the man who visited me in London also had a badly done gold filling, and it was in exactly the same tooth. I noticed it when he laughed about the bet he had made with the Mawson's manager. Suddenly, I was sure that there were not two men, but only one. I've already told you that the two Mr Pinners looked the same except that they had different hair and Mr Arthur Pinner had a beard. And it would be easy for someone to wear a wig to cover their own hair and to shave off a beard, wouldn't it?

'I didn't say anything to Mr Pinner about my suspicions,' Mr Pycroft went on. 'But when I left him, I asked myself some questions. There was obviously only one Mr Pinner. So why had the man sent me from London to Birmingham? Why had he written a letter to himself? Why had he disguised[93] himself and pretended to be two different people? I couldn't think of any answers, but I'd heard of a man who would find them for me. I decided to consult Mr Sherlock Holmes, Dr Watson. I travelled to London very early this morning to tell him what I have now told you.'

'And I am very glad that you consulted me,' Holmes said. 'The case is a very interesting one. I want to meet Mr Pinner very much. Dr Watson and I will come with you when you visit him this evening.'

'Who shall I tell him you are?' asked the young man.

'You must tell him that we are friends of yours who are looking for new jobs. You must say that we are both clerks from London, but we have now decided to move to Birmingham.'

Soon after we had made our plan, the train arrived at Birmingham's New Street Station.

4

Brotherly Love

A little later, Sherlock Holmes, Hall Pycroft and I were walking along Corporation Street when our young friend spoke suddenly. 'That's him!' he said, pointing to a man in front of us. 'That's Harry Pinner!'

We saw a person who was exactly like the one Mr Pycroft had described for us. We watched him buy a newspaper, then we watched him enter number 126. We waited for a few minutes and then we entered the building too. We climbed the stairs to the top floor and Mr Pycroft led us to the Franco-Midland office. He knocked on the door.

'Come in,' said an unhappy voice from inside the room.

We entered the room. Mr Pycroft's employer was sitting at the desk. The newspaper was open in front of him and there was a jug of water on the desk too. The man looked terrible. His face was pale and his hands were shaking. He seemed very frightened and desperately sad at the same time.

'Are you ill, Mr Pinner?' Hall Pycroft asked. 'You don't look well.'

At first I thought that the man at the desk did not recognize our young friend, but he was obviously trying hard to appear normal. 'Ah, it's you, Mr Pycroft,' he said after a moment. 'You are right. I'm not feeling well today. Who are these gentlemen with you?'

Mr Pycroft quickly told him what we had agreed, that we were clerks looking for new jobs.

'Well, it's possible that I might have jobs for your friends later in the year,' said Mr Pinner, when he had heard the young man's story. 'Will you all wait here for a few minutes, please? There's something that I must do.'

He got up and went through the door into the second office. He closed the door behind him.

'Is he trying to escape?' whispered Holmes.

'No, there is no way to get out of that room except back through this one,' Mr Pycroft replied quietly.

'I wonder why he is so frightened,' said Holmes.

'Perhaps he's guessed that we are detectives and that we have discovered his secret,' I said.

'No, Watson, he was frightened before he saw us,' Holmes replied. 'He didn't become pale when we entered – he was already pale.'

At that moment we heard strange noises coming from the next room. There was a noise like coughing and, at the same time, a noise like drumming[94].

'What *is* he doing in there, Holmes?' I asked. 'I don't like those noises!'

We all ran to the door and we tried to open it. But it had been locked from the inside. We kicked it and pushed against it with our shoulders until, at last, the door broke and fell inwards. We entered the room and saw a terrible sight. Mr Pinner was lying on the floor with his belt round his neck. The belt was tight and it was choking[95] him.

We moved quickly. I got hold of the man and held him up. Holmes got a pocket knife from his coat and cut the belt. Then we laid Mr Pinner on the floor again. I listened to his heart and felt the pulse[96] in his wrist. I brought the jug of water from the other room and poured some over his face.

'Will he live, Watson?' Holmes asked. 'Or were we too late to save the poor man?'

'He'll live,' I answered. 'We weren't too late. He'll start to recover soon. But why on earth[P] did he do it?'

'Well, he had obviously planned something criminal,' said Holmes. 'And he obviously thought that his plans were going wrong. We don't know any more than that at the moment.

But I think we must ask the police to investigate this case now. It's a pity – I'd like to give them the complete solution to the puzzle when they arrive.'

'Well, it's certainly a puzzle to me,' young Mr Pycroft said. 'I still don't understand why he brought me here from London. I don't understand why he gave me two completely unnecessary tasks and –'

'Oh, that's quite clear,' said Holmes. 'He brought you here so that you couldn't talk to anyone in London. He gave you a task which kept you here, and stopped you returning there. The clue is the letter that he made you write when he first visited you, I think. He wanted a sample of your handwriting so that someone else could copy it. That someone else is now pretending to be you in London. Pinner obviously needed an accomplice at Mawson's. We don't know why yet.

'The manager at Mawson's never heard from you,' Holmes continued. 'He didn't know that you'd refused his job. He'd never seen you. So when somebody arrived on Monday and said he was Mr Hall Pycroft, the new clerk, the manager must have believed him. The new clerk's writing must have looked like the writing on the letter you sent in answer to their advertisement. Of course the "somebody" had several days to learn how to write like you – to forge your handwriting. But the plan could only work if nobody saw you in London.'

'I've been so stupid,' Mr Pycroft said. 'Everything you say must be true, Mr Holmes, but there is something I still don't understand. Why did Mr Pinner do this to himself as soon as he saw us together?'

At that moment, the man on the floor began to recover. 'The newspaper – the newspaper,' he said in a weak voice.

And when we looked at the newspaper which the man had been reading when we arrived, it explained the final puzzle. On the page he had been reading, there was an article which told us everything.

There has been a terrible murder in London's financial district. This morning a man was found dead in the offices of Mawson and Williams. Mawson's keeps securities worth a large amount of money in its safe at the weekends. The dead man was employed to guard the safe. At one o'clock, a policeman who was passing Mawson's offices was surprised to see a man leaving the building carrying a heavy bag. The policeman knew that the offices close at twelve o'clock on Saturdays, so he tried to stop the man. There was a desperate struggle, but finally the man was arrested. In his bag, the police found securities worth one hundred thousand pounds. And when the police searched the offices, they found the guard dead in the firm's safe. The safe's lock had been broken.

At first, it seemed that the murderer was a new clerk at the firm called Hall Pycroft, who had only worked for the firm for a very short time. But the police have now said that the murderer is really a well-known criminal called Beddington. He was pretending to be Mr Pycroft. This criminal, who is a safebreaker and forger, usually works with his brother. The two men have recently been released from prison. They had been sent to prison for five years. But the man's brother was not with him today. The police are now looking for him.

'And we have found him for them,' said Holmes. 'Even among criminals there is brotherly love and family loyalty. Mr Pinner knew that his brother would be executed for the murder, so he tried to execute himself too. Well, Watson and I will stay with him, Mr Pycroft. Please go and find a policeman.'

A SCANDAL IN BOHEMIA

1

A Royal Visit

I like to call this last case 'A Scandal in Bohemia' although, in the end, a scandal was avoided. In fact, the case wasn't really one of Holmes's successes. But during the case, he met a person who impressed him, which was a rare thing. That person was a woman, which was an even rarer thing. Afterwards, he always called her '*the* woman' or 'the *only* woman'. He still calls her that when we talk about the case, although she is dead now. He rarely uses her name, which was Irene Adler. He was not in love with her. There has never been any room in Holmes's logical mind for love. The woman impressed him because she defeated[97] him. At last, he said, he had met someone who was as intelligent and logical as him ...

One evening, I visited Holmes in Baker Street. He still lived there, in the flat I had shared with him before I was married. As soon as I arrived, he showed me a letter.

> *Mr Sherlock Holmes,*
> *Tonight, at a quarter to eight, you will be visited by a gentleman. He has heard about your great skill as a detective. He has also heard about your great discretion – he knows that you can be trusted with secrets. He wishes to consult you about a serious problem. The problem must be solved with great discretion. The gentleman will be wearing a mask on his face. Please do not be offended[98] by this. Please be at home when he comes.*

There was no signature.

'What does this strange note tell you, Watson?' Holmes asked me.

I tried to be as logical as my friend. 'Well, the first thing I noticed is that the writing paper is very unusual,' I said. 'And it must be very expensive.'

'You're right, Watson,' said Holmes. 'The writing paper *is* unusual. It isn't British paper. Hold it up to the light and look carefully at it.'

The light showed that there was a watermark in the paper – the name of a famous German paper-maker followed by a monogram. The monogram was formed by two letters twisted together – a large 'E' and a small 'g'.

'What does the monogram stand for, Holmes?' I asked. 'Does it stand for the writer's name?'

'No,' he replied. 'It stands for "Egria", a German-speaking country in Bohemia. I think that our masked visitor must be from that country. And I think that we are about to meet him.'

As he spoke, we heard footsteps on the stairs outside Holmes's door. A moment later someone knocked on the door and entered the room. It was a man – a very large man, who was at least six and a half feet tall. The top part of his face was covered with a black mask, and he was carrying a wide hat. There was fur on the collar of his coat and round the tops of his boots. Over his coat he wore a cloak fastened[99] with a brooch made of gold with a single large jewel in the centre. The man's clothes told us that he was very rich, and that he was not an Englishman.

'I hope you got my note,' he said. He had a strong German accent.

'Yes, I got it,' said Holmes. 'Please sit down. This is my colleague, Dr Watson, who helps me with my work. And what is your name, sir?'

'You may call me Count von Kramm,' the large man said as he sat down. 'I am a Bohemian aristocrat[100]. I hope you will

The top part of his face was covered with a black mask, and he was carrying a wide hat.

excuse my mask. The royal person that I represent[101] today wishes me to be unknown to you. In fact, the name I just gave you is not really my own name.'

'Yes,' said Holmes again. 'I know that.'

The man paused for a moment in surprise. Then he went on.

'Have you heard of the Ormstein family, Mr Holmes?' he said. 'The kings of Bohemia have always been Ormsteins. The royal person needs to consult you about a serious problem for the great Ormstein family.'

'Yes, I know that too,' Holmes said. 'And I've known since you entered the room that you are Wilhelm Sigismond von Ormstein, Duke of Cassel and King of Bohemia. If you will tell me what your problem is, your Majesty, I will tell you if I can help you.'

The man jumped up and walked quickly around the room. He was obviously anxious, and he was obviously trying to make a decision. Finally he took off his mask.

'You are right,' he said. 'I am the king. Why should I hide it from you? But I have travelled secretly from Prague to consult you. Nobody in my country knows that I am in London. Nobody must find out that I have come here.'

'We will keep your secret. Now, please sit down and tell us what has happened,' Holmes said.

The man sat down and told us his story.

2

The Problem

'Five years ago,' he began, 'I was in Warsaw, in Poland, for several months. I got to know a woman called Irene Adler there. She was an opera singer. She was very beautiful. I know now that she likes men to fall in love with her. She likes the power that this gives her. But I was a young man then and I did not understand that.'

'Wait one moment, please,' Holmes said. 'Find the entry for Irene Adler in my index, Watson,' he told me.

On a bookshelf behind me were the large notebooks of Holmes's 'index'. The books contained notes on hundreds of people that Holmes was interested in. The entries were arranged alphabetically, by name. I took down the first book and quickly found the entry that Holmes wanted. I gave him the book.

'Irene Adler,' he read. 'She was born in New Jersey, USA. She was the chief female singer of the opera companies in Milan and Warsaw. She has now retired from the opera companies, but she still gives concerts. And I see that she now lives in London.'

Holmes put down the notebook and looked at the king. 'Well, I think I can guess what happened, your Majesty,' he said. 'You were in love with Irene Adler for a while. You wrote her some indiscreet[102] letters. And you now want those letters back. Am I right?'

'Yes. But how did you know ...?' the king began.

'Was there a secret marriage?' Holmes went on. 'Is she your legal wife?'

'No,' the king replied. 'There are no legal papers which can link her to me.'

'What is the problem, then?' Holmes said. 'If she tries to blackmail[103] you by making the letters public, you can say that they are forgeries. You can say that she has asked someone to steal your writing paper and a sample of your handwriting, and Miss Adler has copied it.'

'If she only had letters, I could say that,' the king replied. 'But she has a photograph too.'

'Anyone can buy a photograph of you,' Holmes said. 'That doesn't prove anything.'

'But we are *both* in the photograph,' the king said sadly. '*That* is the problem.'

'Ah!' said Holmes. 'You *have* been indiscreet. That is very serious.'

'I was young and I was stupid then,' the king said. 'And I was only a prince. Now I am thirty and I am the king. I must protect my family's honour.'

'Have you tried to buy the photograph back?' asked Holmes.

'Yes, but she will not sell it,' the king replied.

'Well, we must steal it,' Holmes said. 'That is the only way to help you.'

'Mr Holmes, my servants have already tried to steal it,' the king said. 'They have tried five times. They broke into her house when she was out and searched it. They arranged for Miss Adler's luggage to be lost when she was travelling by train. They searched the luggage. They attacked her carriage on the road and searched her. It is a large photograph, but they can never find it. She has hidden it well. And now she wants to use it to ruin my life.'

'How will she do that?' Holmes asked.

'I am going to be married soon,' the king replied. 'I am going to marry Princess Clotilde, the daughter of the King of Scandinavia. I want her to be my queen. But if her father finds out that I once loved Irene Adler, he will not allow the marriage.'

'I understand. You are going to be married and Miss Adler is jealous,' Holmes said.

'Yes. She has told me that if I do not marry *her*, she will not let me marry anyone else,' the king replied.

'Why hasn't Miss Adler made the photograph public already?' Holmes asked.

'She is waiting until the day when the date of my marriage is announced to the world,' the king said. 'On that day, the King of Scandinavia will learn about the photograph. And that day will be Monday.'

'That gives us three days,' said Holmes calmly. 'Well, I need to know three things. First, where are you staying in London, your Majesty?'

'At the Langham Hotel,' said the king. 'I am staying there under the name of Count von Kramm.'

'We will contact you there when we have some news,' said Holmes. 'Second, what is the lady's address?'

'She lives in a house in St John's Wood, in north London,' said the king. 'The house is called Briony Lodge.'

'And third, do you understand that I might have to spend a lot of money to get your photograph back?' Holmes said.

'Money is not a problem,' the king replied. 'Spend as much as you need to spend.'

Before he left, the king gave Holmes a bag containing one thousand pounds.

3

The Witness at a Wedding

When I arrived at Baker Street the next afternoon, Holmes was not at home. I sat down to wait for him and after an hour I heard footsteps on the stairs. The door opened and a very shabby[104] man entered, whose clothes were old and torn. His face was red and he looked as if he drank too much. He was dressed like the kind of man who takes care of horses – a groom. Holmes's skill at disguising himself had been useful in many of his cases. So I was not surprised when the 'groom' went into Holmes's bedroom. And I was not surprised when my friend came out of the room a few minutes later, looking as smart as usual.

He sat down in his chair and he laughed happily.

'I've been a witness at a wedding, Watson,' he said when he had finished laughing. 'Let me tell you about it.

'This morning, I went to look at Irene Adler's house in St John's Wood. It's a small house with a garden behind it and no garden in front of it. The front of the house is next to the street. The windows of the house are large with the usual English kind of lock and they are quite easy to open from the outside. It will be simple to break into the house if we have to do that.

'There is a row of buildings next to the garden where people keep their horses and their carriages,' Holmes continued. 'I talked to some of the grooms there and they were very indiscreet. London grooms are never discreet, Watson. After I had bought them something to drink, they were very willing to tell me about Irene Adler. They're all in love with her, of course! I learnt that she doesn't leave her house very often in the mornings, except if she is going to sing at a concert.

But she always goes out in the afternoon, between five and seven o'clock, to drive in Regent's Park. I learnt that she is often visited at home by a gentleman. The gentleman visits Briony Lodge every day, sometimes twice a day, and he is her only male visitor. And I learnt that the gentleman is a lawyer and that his name is Mr Godfrey Norton. He is a dark-haired, handsome man with important friends, the grooms told me.

'That news worried me a little, Watson,' Holmes said. 'If Mr Norton was her lawyer, I told myself, she had probably given him the photograph, to keep it in his safe. But if he was her lover, I thought, it was unlikely that he knew about the photograph. It was unlikely that he knew about her friendship with the king at all. So I hoped that he was her lover.

'After I'd talked to the grooms, I watched the street in front of the house for a while,' he went on. 'Soon a cab stopped by Briony Lodge and a man got out. I knew he was Godfrey Norton because he was exactly like the man the grooms had described. He went into the house. I could see him through the windows as he talked to someone inside. He seemed very anxious and he was waving his arms about. I didn't see Miss Adler herself. The man didn't stay very long and when he came out again, I heard the words he spoke to the driver of his cab. He asked to be taken to the shop of a famous jeweller, and then to St Monica's Church in Edgware Road. He said that he had to be at the church in twenty minutes.

'Soon after he left, a small carriage arrived at the house. Irene Adler came out and got into it. Good heavens, she's a lovely woman, Watson! She also asked her driver to take her to St Monica's Church. And she also had to be there in twenty minutes. You can guess what I thought was going to happen.

'I quickly found a cab and I followed the carriage,' Holmes said. 'When I arrived at the church, there was no one outside, so I went in. Miss Adler and Mr Norton were talking to a clergyman[105] at the far end of the church, so I sat down near the door to watch them. But after a minute, Mr Norton saw me and came towards me. "You're going to help me," he said firmly. "Do you understand?" He thought that I was a poor groom and he wasn't polite. "You must be a witness for me," he said. "I'm getting married. And I can't get married without a witness." Well, I did my duty[P]. The two of them got married and I was the witness. Then they agreed to meet again late this evening and they left the church separately.

'So that was my morning's work, Watson,' Holmes finished. 'Irene Adler is now Mrs Norton, and I was a witness at her wedding.

'We must act quickly now, Watson,' he said. 'Mr and Mrs Norton might leave London soon for a holiday after the wedding. We must recover the king's photograph before they leave. Will you help me?'

'Of course I'll help you,' I replied.

'Are you willing to break the law?' he asked.

'If it is broken for a good reason, then yes, I will break the law,' I said.

'Listen carefully, then,' said Holmes. 'This evening we will go to St John's Wood together. I will leave you a short distance from Briony Lodge. You must watch what happens after that, but you mustn't interfere[106] in it. Do you understand? You must only watch. Something unpleasant will happen to me, but you mustn't try to help me. I will be taken into the house. You must then come near to the house and stand by the left-hand window. Soon the window will be opened and you'll see me inside the room. When you see me raise my hand, you must throw *this* through the window.'

As he spoke, he took a small smoke bomb from his pocket and gave it to me. 'Now I must change my clothes, and after that we must go to St John's Wood,' he went on. 'I'll tell you more about my plan on the way.'

4

A Fight in the Street

At a little before seven o'clock that evening, we arrived in the district of St John's Wood. That district of London is not far from Baker Street and we arrived on foot. Holmes was disguised as a clergyman. He could have been a fine actor if he had not become a detective! As we walked towards Briony Lodge, he told me his plan.

'I'm sure that the photograph is hidden in a secret place in the house,' he said. 'It's too large for Irene Adler to carry it with her everywhere. But the king's servants couldn't find it when they broke in. It must be very cleverly hidden. The woman has two reasons to hide it now. She wants to keep it safe so that she can blackmail the king. But she doesn't want her new husband to know about it either.'

'How will you find it, then, Holmes?' I asked. 'She won't tell you where it is, even if she thinks you are an innocent clergyman.'

'It's simple. I'll make her *show* me where it is, Watson,' he replied.

'But how will you do that?' I said.

'I understand the minds of women like Irene Adler,' he replied. 'If a married woman's house catches fire, the first thing that she will try to save is her baby. If a rich *un*married woman's house catches fire, she will probably try to save her jewels first. But Irene Adler will want to save the thing that gives her power. I believe that the photograph is the first thing that she will try to save if her house catches fire. So we'll make her think that it *has* caught fire. I'll get into the house, in the way that I've planned. You'll throw the smoke bomb. When your bomb starts to release smoke, shout "Fire! The house is burning!" Then walk quickly to the corner of the street and wait for me. I'll join you there after ten minutes.

'When you shout, some other people in the street will start to shout too,' Holmes went on. 'I shall be watching Irene Adler carefully. I hope that she will give away her secret. Do you remember Jonas Oldacre, the Norwood Builder, Watson? A fire that we started made him give away *his* secret, didn't it?'

We stopped about a hundred yards away from Briony Lodge. There were already several men near the house. Holmes said, 'Ah, there are my friends. You must stay here for now, Watson.' And he walked on towards them. Two of the men were soldiers. Two were rich young men in expensive clothes, who were calling to a pretty young woman on the other side of the street. Some other shabby men were doing nothing at all. They were just looking at the sky.

Then, as I watched, something very strange happened. As Holmes reached the house, a small carriage approached and stopped in front of it. A very beautiful woman got out of it. At that moment, a fight broke out between two of the men in the street. Soon all the others joined in and the woman from the carriage was caught in the middle of the fight. But there was something unreal about the scene – I felt as if I was watching a play. And then Holmes tried to interfere in the fight, trying to protect the woman.

In a moment, all the men started to attack Holmes instead of each other. He shouted for help, but I did not interfere. He quickly fell to the ground and I saw blood on his face. Then suddenly all the men ran away. At the same time the woman and her driver went to help Holmes.

'Will you get me some water, please?' Holmes said to the woman, in a weak voice.

'Please come into my house,' she replied. 'You must lie down until you feel better.'

As they entered the house, I moved carefully towards the left-hand window. Five minutes later, I saw a servant open it. I saw Holmes inside the room. He raised his hand, and then he moved quickly away from the open window. I threw the smoke bomb through the window and I shouted, 'Fire! Fire! The house is burning!' As I ran towards the corner, the street filled with people again. They were shouting too.

When Holmes joined me ten minutes later, he was smiling.

'Well, I know where the photograph is now,' he said.

'What happened?' I asked. 'Tell me everything, Holmes.'

'All the men in the street were actors, of course,' he went on. 'I paid them earlier this afternoon and told them what to do. The blood on my face came from the theatre too – it wasn't real. When Mrs Norton and her driver got me inside the house, I lay on a sofa in the sitting room. Mrs Norton went to get me some water and I asked a servant to open the window. You threw the bomb and shouted, and the woman hurried back into the room. She ran to a corner where the wall was made of wooden panels. There's a secret cupboard behind a wooden panel there, disguised as part of the wall. She opened it and began to take something out. Then she saw the smoke bomb and she quickly put the thing back and closed the panel. She left the room quickly, without speaking, and I left the house. Her driver was watching me so I didn't steal the photograph.'

As we walked home, Holmes told me the rest of his plan.

'I'll send the king a message tonight,' he said. 'Tomorrow morning, we'll call at Briony Lodge with the king. We'll arrive early, before Mrs Norton has got dressed. The servants will tell us to wait in the sitting room until she is ready to see us. We'll open the secret panel and take the photograph. I hope we won't see the lady at all. If we do, we'll give her a problem. We'll say that we'll tell her husband what we know about her if she tries to make trouble.'

'There's a secret cupboard behind a wooden panel there, disguised as part of the wall. She opened it and began to take something out.'

It seemed like a good plan. We were pleased with our day's work when we reached Baker Street. But one strange thing happened that evening. When we arrived at Holmes's door, a slim young man passed us in the street.

'Goodnight, Mr Sherlock Holmes,' he said quietly. Then he walked quickly away.

'Who was that?' said Holmes. 'I'm sure I've heard that voice before.'

5

A Shock for Holmes

Holmes, the king and I travelled to St John's Wood in a carriage early the next morning. On the way, Holmes told the king that Irene Adler was now married. It was obviously a terrible shock for him.

'Are you sure about that? When did she marry? And who did she marry?' the king asked angrily.

'She married a lawyer called Godfrey Norton, and she married him yesterday morning,' Holmes replied. 'And I'm quite sure. I was there.'

'Ah, she cannot love him,' the king said. 'She loved only me. She will never love anyone else.' It was obvious that his feelings were hurt.

'I hope that she loves him, Your Majesty,' Holmes said. 'If she loves *him*, then she doesn't love *you*. And that means that she probably won't try to interfere with your marriage plans. But we can't be sure about it. We must still recover the photograph.'

The king looked unhappy. 'She is so beautiful,' he said. 'I wish she had been an aristocrat. She would have been a wonderful queen for me.'

It was eight o'clock when we arrived at Briony Lodge. An elderly servant opened the door.

'I think that one of you gentlemen is Mr Sherlock Holmes,' she said. 'Mrs Norton told me you were coming. But she isn't here. She and her husband left at five o'clock this morning. They've gone to Europe and will never return.'

We hurried past the servant, into the house. In the sitting room, all the furniture had been moved and the secret cupboard was open. Holmes ran to it. He put his hand into it and searched it. When he took his hand out again he was holding a large photograph – but it was a photograph of Irene Adler. He was also holding a letter, which was addressed to him.

He opened the envelope and read the contents. If the king had had a shock, Holmes now had one too. He showed the letter to the king and then to me.

Dear Mr Holmes,
You did very well. You made me give away my secret. I knew, months ago, that if the king was desperate he would consult you. I was expecting you to come. But you still deceived me with your clever disguise and your excellent actors. I have been on the stage myself, of course. I know about acting. But you were very good. I only understood that the clergyman was really Mr Sherlock Holmes when I saw the smoke bomb. Even then, I needed to be sure. I dressed as a boy and took a cab to Baker Street. I saw the clergyman stop outside the house where the famous detective lives. I even said goodnight to you.

Please tell the king not to worry. I am now married to a better man than he will ever be. I still have the photograph, but I won't make it public unless he tries to make trouble for me.

Yours very sincerely,
Irene Norton, formerly Irene Adler

Before we left him that morning, Holmes asked the king if he could have the photograph of Irene Adler. He still keeps it in his sitting room. 'What a woman!' Holmes says, if I ever mention her name.

Points For Understanding

THE NORWOOD BUILDER

1

1 What facts did Sherlock Holmes know about McFarlane? How did he know?
2 What reasons did the newspaper article give to show that the police believed Mr Oldacre had been murdered?

2

1 How did Holmes know that the draft of the will had been written on an express train?

3

1 Why did Holmes say that Lestrade might be right that McFarlane was guilty?

4

1 What was the result of the fire which Watson lit?
2 How did Holmes work out what really happened in this case?
3 What have you learnt in this story about the relationship between Lestrade and Holmes?

THE SECOND STAIN

1

1 What have you learnt about Holmes's two important visitors?
2 Why should the letter have been safe?

2

1 Why was the letter so important?

3

1 Who was Eduardo Lucas, and why did Holmes think he was important?
2 What have you learnt about Lady Hilda Hope?

4

1 Who was Madame Fournaye? Did Holmes think she was important?
2 What did Holmes think was the most important thing that had happened in the previous three days?

5

1 What was the puzzle which Lestrade wanted to show Holmes?
2 Who had moved the carpet, and why?

6

1 How did Holmes make Lady Hilda admit that she had the letter?

7

1 Why did Lady Hilda steal the letter?
2 Holmes did not tell Trelawney Hope and the Prime Minister what really happened. Do you think that he was right not to tell them?

THE STOCKBROKER'S CLERK

1

1 What have you learnt about Hall Pycroft?

2

1 Why was Hall Pycroft worried about taking the job with the Franco-Midland Hardware Company? Why did he decide to take it?
2 What strange thing did Arthur Pinner ask Hall Pycroft to do?
3 Arthur Pinner described his meeting with the Mawson's manager. Why did it make Hall Pycroft angry?

3

1 What worried Hall Pycroft about the Franco-Midland Hardware Company's office?
2 What happened to shock Hall Pycroft?

4

1 How did Holmes and Watson save Mr Pinner?
2 Why did Holmes think that Mr Pinner had brought Hall Pycroft to Birmingham? How did he guess this?
3 What was the crime which the brothers were trying to carry out?

A SCANDAL IN BOHEMIA

1

1 Why was Holmes impressed by Irene Adler?
2 What have you learnt about Holmes's visitor?

2

1 What was the king's problem?

3

1 What did Holmes learn about Irene Adler from the grooms?
2 What did Holmes have to do in the church?

4

1 Holmes had a plan to make Irene Adler show him where she had hidden the photograph. What was his plan?
2 What arrangements did Holmes make to get taken into Irene Adler's house?
3 What strange thing happened as Holmes and Watson arrived at Holmes's door in Baker Street?

5

1 Why was this case not a success for Holmes?

Glossary

1 ***published*** – *to publish something* (page 4)
to have something that you have written printed and sold

2 ***emotion*** (page 4)
a feeling that you experience, for example love, fear or anger

3 ***logical*** (page 4)
connecting ideas or reasons in a sensible way

4 ***solving*** – *to solve something* (page 4)
to find the reason or explanation for something. A way to solve a problem or to deal with a bad situation is called a *solution*.

5 ***based*** – *to base something on something* (page 4)
to use something as a model for a film, piece of writing or work of art

6 ***although*** (page 6)
used for introducing a statement that gives new information about what you have just said

7 ***case*** (page 7)
a crime that the police are trying to solve, or a problem that someone has

8 ***investigated*** – *to investigate something* (page 7)
to try to find out the facts about something in order to learn the truth about it

9 ***obviously*** (page 7)
in a way that is clear for almost anyone to see or understand

10 ***code*** (page 8)
a system of words, numbers or signs used for sending messages

11 ***legal*** (page 8)
relating to the law or lawyers

12 ***sealed*** – *to seal something* (page 8)
to close an envelope by sticking down the top edge. Sometimes, *sealing wax* – a hard substance that becomes like a liquid when you heat it – is used to make a *seal*. You have to break it before you can open a letter, document, etc.

13 ***consulting*** (page 10)
providing professional help and advice about a particular subject

14 ***arrested*** – *to arrest someone* (page 10)
if the police *arrest* someone, they take that person to a police station because they believe he or she has committed a crime

15 ***puzzle*** (page 10)
something that is very difficult to understand

16 ***rushed*** – *to rush* (page 11)
to hurry in order to get somewhere very quickly

17 ***desperately*** (page 11)
in a very worried or angry way

18 ***scandal*** (page 11)
talk or reports in the newspapers about shocking events involving important people

19 ***charge*** – *to charge someone (with something)* (page 11)
to accuse someone officially of committing a crime. If you *commit* a crime, you do something legally wrong.

20 ***fierce*** (page 12)
very angry, or ready to attack

21 ***lung*** (page 12)
one of the two organs in your chest that fill with air when you breathe

22 ***searching*** – *to search for someone or something* (page 12)
to try to find something or someone by looking carefully

23 ***suspect*** (page 12)
someone who the police believe may have committed a crime. If someone *suspects* someone of something, they believe that someone has done something, usually something bad.

24 ***district*** (page 12)
one of the areas into which a town or country is divided for official purposes

25 ***firm*** (page 12)
a business or company

26 ***except for*** (page 12)
used for introducing the only person, thing or fact that is not included in your main statement

27 ***housekeeper*** (page 13)
someone whose job is to clean someone else's house and sometimes cook their meals

28 ***timber store*** (page 13)
a *store* is a place where a supply of something is kept until it is needed. *Timber* is wood used for building houses or making furniture.

29 ***safe*** (page 13)
a strong metal box with a special lock, used for storing valuable things

30 ***mark*** (page 13)
a damaged or dirty area on the surface of something

31 ***flesh*** (page 13)
the soft part of people's or animals' bodies that consists mostly of muscle and fat

32 ***protect*** – *to protect someone or something* (page 14)
to keep someone or something safe from harm, injury, damage or loss

33 ***evidence*** (page 15)
facts, statements or objects that help to prove whether or not someone has committed a crime

34 ***trial*** (page 15)
the process of examining a case in a court of law and deciding whether someone is guilty or innocent

35 ***will*** (page 15)
a legal document that explains what you want to happen to your money and possessions after you die

36 ***draft*** (page 15)
something such as a plan, letter or drawing that may have changes made to it before it is finished

37 ***clerk*** (page 16)
someone whose job is to look after the documents in an office, court, etc.

38 ***witness*** (page 16)
someone who watches you sign an official document and then signs it to state that they have watched you

39 ***proof*** (page 16)
information or evidence that shows that something is definitely true or definitely exists. If you provide information or evidence that something is true, you *prove* it.

40 ***points*** (page 16)
a place on a railway line where the tracks on which trains travel can be moved so that a train can change from one track to another

41 ***express train*** (page 17)
a train that makes a particular journey more quickly than an ordinary train, usually because it stops at fewer stations

42 ***bloodstain*** (page 22)
a *stain* is a mark left accidentally on clothes or surfaces. A *bloodstain* is a mark made accidentally by blood.

43 ***fingerprint*** (page 22)
a mark that you leave on something when you touch it, showing the pattern of lines on the skin of your fingers

44 ***paced*** – *to pace (up and down)* (page 22)
to walk with regular steps, because you are measuring something or because you are worried or impatient

45 ***straw*** (page 23)
the yellow stems of dried crops such as wheat

46 ***shed*** (page 23)
a small building, usually made of wood, in which you store things

47 ***bucket*** (page 23)
a round open container with a handle, used for carrying liquid and substances such as sand or soil

48 ***clue*** (page 24)
an object or fact that someone discovers that helps them solve a crime or mystery

49 ***measured*** – *to measure something* (page 26)
to find the exact size, amount, speed, etc. of something, usually using a special tool or special equipment but here with your footsteps

50 ***diplomatic*** (page 28)
relating to the profession or skill of preserving or creating friendly relationships between countries

51 ***reputation*** (page 28)
the opinion that people have about how good or how bad someone or something is

52 ***Minister*** (page 28)
an official in charge of a government department in the UK and some other countries. Ministers work in a government department called a *ministry*.

53 ***dispatch box*** (page 29)
a red case that a minister in the British government uses for carrying documents

54 ***unguarded*** (page 30)
an *unguarded* place or object is not watched or protected by anyone

55 ***valet*** (page 30)
a man whose job is to look after another man's clothes and be his personal assistant
56 ***trust*** – *to trust someone* (page 30)
to be confident that someone is honest, fair and reliable
57 ***despair*** (page 30)
the feeling that a situation is so bad that nothing you can do will change it
58 ***deduction*** (page 31)
the process of finding something out by considering the information or evidence that you have
59 ***policy*** (page 32)
a set of plans or actions agreed on by a government, political party, business or other group
60 ***empire*** (page 32)
a number of countries ruled by one person or government
61 ***pretend*** (page 32)
to behave in a particular way because you want someone to believe that something is true when it is not
62 ***shocking*** (page 32)
something that is *shocking* makes you feel extremely surprised or upset
63 ***accusation*** (page 32)
a claim that someone has done something illegal or wrong
64 ***rival*** (page 32)
a person, team or business that competes with another
65 ***groaned*** – *to groan* (page 32)
to make a long low sound, for example because you are in pain or unhappy
66 ***ruined*** – *to ruin something* (page 32)
to destroy or severely damage something
67 ***burglary*** (page 35)
the crime of entering a building illegally in order to steal things. Someone who commits this crime is a *burglar*.

68 ***coincidence*** (page 35)
a situation in which separate things happen by chance at the same time or in the same way

69 ***accomplice*** (page 36)
someone who helps another person to do something illegal or wrong

70 ***Lady*** (page 36)
in the UK, the title *Lady* is used for women who have an important social position. Lady Hilda Hope's father was a duke, which is why she has the title *Lady*.

71 ***inquest*** (page 38)
an official attempt by a court to find the cause of someone's death

72 ***jury*** (page 38)
a group of people, usually twelve, who judge a court case. Members of a *jury* are ordinary members of the public.

73 ***prosecution*** (page 38)
the process or act of accusing someone of a crime and asking a court of law to judge them. If you accuse someone of a crime and ask a court of law to judge them, you *prosecute* them.

74 ***release*** (page 38)
to let someone leave a place where they have been kept

75 ***suspicious*** (page 39)
making you believe that something is wrong, dangerous or illegal

76 ***confront*** (page 40)
to speak to someone in a very direct way, because you disagree with them and you want them to explain their opinions or behaviour

77 ***block*** (page 41)
a solid piece of wood, stone, ice, etc. with straight sides

78 ***examine*** (page 42)
to look at something carefully in order to find out about it or see what it is like

79 ***foolish*** (page 44)
not behaving in an intelligent or sensible way. Someone who is *foolish* is a *fool.*

80 ***public house*** (page 44)
a *pub* – a place where people go to have a drink, especially in the UK and Ireland

81 ***brandy*** (page 44)
a strong drink made from wine. It was often used as medicine at the time when the stories were written.

82 ***twisted*** (page 44)
bent into a shape that is not normal

83 ***insulted*** – *to insult someone* (page 46)
to say or do something that shows a lack of respect for someone

84 ***butler*** (page 46)
the most important male servant in a rich person's house, whose job is to organize the other servants, to welcome guests, to pour wine at meals, etc.

85 ***luncheon*** (page 47)
a formal word for *lunch* – a meal that you eat in the middle of the day

86 ***stockbroker*** (page 52)
someone whose job is to buy and sell *shares* – equal parts of a company that people can buy as a way of investing money. A *stockbroker* works in the *stock market.*

87 ***cheated*** – *to cheat someone* (page 53)
to treat someone dishonestly

88 ***deal in*** – *to deal in something* (page 53)
to buy and sell something

89 ***securities*** (page 53)
documents showing that you own shares in a company

90 ***word of mouth*** (page 56)
communication that consists of comments that people make to each other in an informal way, not formal communication such as letters, news reports or advertisements

91 ***bet*** (page 56)
if you *bet* on something, you risk an amount of money by saying what you think will happen, especially in a race or game. You lose the money if you are wrong and win more if you are right. Someone who *makes a bet* risks money in this way.

92 ***poverty*** (page 57)
a situation in which someone does not have enough money to pay for their basic needs

93 ***disguised*** – *to disguise oneself* (page 61)
to make changes in the way you look so that other people will not recognize you

94 ***drumming*** (page 64)
the sound of something repeatedly hitting a surface

95 ***choking*** – *to choke someone* (page 64)
to squeeze someone's neck so they cannot breathe

96 ***pulse*** (page 64)
the regular movement of blood as the heart pumps it round the body

97 ***defeated*** – *to defeat someone* (page 67)
to win against someone in a game, fight or competition

98 ***offended*** (page 67)
upset or angry because of something that someone has said or done

99 ***fastened*** – *to fasten something* (page 68)
to close something such as a piece of clothing or a bag, usually using the buttons, zip, clip, etc. on it, but here with the pin on a piece of jewellery

100 ***aristocrat*** (page 68)
a member of the *aristocracy* – the people in the highest class of society, who usually have money, land and power, and who often have special titles, such as *countess* or *duke*

101 ***represent*** – *to represent someone* (page 70)
to speak or act officially for another person, group or organization

102 ***indiscreet*** (page 71)
showing a lack of good judgement, especially in talking about things that are intended to be private

103 ***blackmail*** – *to blackmail someone* (page 72)
to make someone give you money or do what you want by threatening to tell people embarrassing information about them

104 ***shabby*** (page 74)
dressed in clothes that are old or in bad condition

105 ***clergyman*** (page 75)
a man who leads religious services in Christian churches

106 ***interfere*** – *to interfere (in something)* (page 76)
to deliberately become involved in a situation and try to influence the way that it develops

Useful Phrases

break my poor mother's heart – *to break someone's heart* (page 11)
to upset someone very much, especially by doing something bad or by letting them know that you do not love them

fear the worst – *to fear the worst* (page 13)
to fear that something very bad has happened to someone or that they could be dead

be kind enough – *will you be kind enough to do something* (page 15)
used for asking someone to do something in a very polite and formal way

wasting your time – *to waste your time on something* (page 19)
to spend your time doing something that cannot or does not produce results

broke off the engagement – *to break off an engagement* (page 20)
to end an agreement to get married

take revenge – *to take revenge on someone* (page 26)
to hurt or punish someone because they have hurt you or someone else

be made public – *to make something public* (page 29)
to tell everyone about something so that it is not private or secret anymore

make trouble – *to make trouble for someone or something* (page 29)
to do or say something that causes someone problems, worries or difficulties

having his own way – *to have your own way* (page 31)
to be allowed to have or do what you want

men of honour – *a man of honour* (page 31)
someone who always behaves in a morally correct way

be greatly to the advantage of – *to be to someone's advantage* (page 32)
to make someone more likely to succeed

I will do my best for you – *to do your best for someone* (page 33)
to try as hard as you can in order to help someone

What do you make of that? – *to make something of something* (page 42)
to understand someone or the meaning of something in a particular way. *What do you make of that?* is used in an informal way for asking someone for their opinion about something.

Good heavens (page 45)
used for adding emphasis to exclamations

My surprise must have been written on my face – *to have something written on your face* (page 59)
used for saying that the expression on your face shows what you are feeling or thinking

Rome wasn't built in a day (page 59)
used for saying that important things often take a long time to do

why on earth ...? (page 64)
used for adding emphasis to questions

I did my duty – *to do your duty* (page 76)
to do something that you are legally or morally obliged to do

Exercises

Background Information

Read 'A Note About The Author' and 'A Note About The Stories'. Write T (True), F (False) or NG (Not Given).

1 Arthur Conan Doyle was Scottish. *T*

2 Conan Doyle was born in the twentieth century. ....

3 Conan Doyle had another profession before becoming a writer. ....

4 The Sherlock Holmes stories were historical stories, set in a time before Conan Doyle lived. ....

5 Conan Doyle's university teacher, Dr Bell, enjoyed the Sherlock Holmes stories. ....

6 Sherlock Holmes stories have been published in both magazines and books. ....

7 Conan Doyle, like Sherlock Holmes, was not an emotional person. ....

8 After a break, Conan Doyle started writing more Sherlock Holmes stories because his readers asked for more. ....

9 In the final Sherlock Holmes story, the detective was killed in Switzerland. ....

10 Conan Doyle did not have any children with his second wife. ....

11 Other writers, apart from Conan Doyle, have written Sherlock Holmes stories. ....

12 A recent film of Sherlock Holmes stars Guy Ritchie as the detective. ....

13 The narrator in the Sherlock Holmes stories is the detective, Sherlock Holmes, himself. ....

14 Dr Watson is Sherlock Holmes's more intelligent assistant, who helps him understand the truth when they investigate cases. ....

15 At the time of the earlier Sherlock Holmes stories, telegrams and letters were the usual ways of communicating messages. ....

16 Conan Doyle did not agree with using the death penalty as a punishment for murderers. ....

Multiple Choice

Choose which story or stories the following sentences refer to. Write 1 (The Norwood Builder), 2 (The Second Stain), 3 (The Stockbroker's Clerk) or 4 (A Scandal in Bohemia).

1 A criminal wanted to take revenge on someone who had refused to marry him thirty years earlier. ....*1*....

2 Holmes made someone believe there was a fire, to help him solve the case. (2 stories) ....

3 No one was murdered. (2 stories) ....

4 Holmes was not successful in finding the photo he had been asked to find. ....

5 Holmes helped to save his country and keep peace in Europe. ....

6 A criminal pretended to be someone else so he could rob a company safe. ....

7 A criminal tried to kill himself. ....

8 Holmes disguised himself as a clergyman in order to enter someone's house. ....

9 Holmes helped a member of a royal family with his marriage plans. ....

10 The wife of a politician exchanged an important letter for one that she had written to another man. ....

11 Someone used wax to help him/her with a plan. (2 stories) ....

12 An important letter was hidden under the floorboards.

....

13 When he was arrested, a criminal pretended that his crime was just a joke. ....

14 Holmes paid people to pretend to attack him. ....

15 Someone wrote a letter to accept an unusual job offer in a city outside London. ....

16 Holmes was a witness at a wedding. ....

17 Some blood on a carpet helped Holmes to find a hiding place. ....

18 A Frenchwoman murdered the man she loved because she was jealous. ....

19 Someone had built a hidden room at the end of a corridor. ....

20 A policeman allowed a beautiful woman to enter the scene of a crime. ....

21 Someone became suspicious because of a gold tooth. ....

22 Holmes was impressed by a woman who was as intelligent and logical as him. ....

Vocabulary: Crime and the law

Complete the gaps. Use each word in the box once.

accomplice alibi blackmail burglary charged
committed evidence ~~executed~~ forge
investigate jury legal proved trial

1 At the time of the Sherlock Holmes stories, murderers were usually punished for their crime by being ....*executed*........ . This was known as the death penalty.

2 Holmes preferred to .... cases which were difficult to solve.

3 The police .... McFarlane with the murder of Oldacre, but Holmes later .... that he did not kill him.

4 Lestrade told Holmes that the bloodstained fingerprint on the wall was .... that McFarlane was the murderer.

5 Lestrade was certain that McFarlane was guilty and that he would soon be on .... for the murder.

6 As nothing in Edward Lucas's house had been stolen, the police did not believe that .... was the reason for the crime.

7 Mitton had a strong .... for the night of Edward Lucas's murder – he had been with friends in another part of London, so he could not have .... the crime.

8 At the inquest on Edward Lucas's death, the .... decided that murder was the cause of his death, but they could not identify the killer.

9 Mr Pinner's brother was his ...., and they worked together to plan and carry out the crime at Mawson's.

10 Beddington had learnt how to .... Hall Pycroft's handwriting so that the manager at Mawson's believed he was Hall Pycroft.

11 Although there were no .... papers, such as a marriage document, to link the king to Irene, the photo of them together could cause a scandal.

12 Irene Adler might use the photo of herself with the king in order to .... him.

Vocabulary: Business, finance and work

Complete the gaps. Use each word in the box once.

applied ~~clerk~~ colleagues dealt financial firm manager securities shares stock market

Hall Pycroft had been working as a (1) ..... *clerk* ..... in London's (2) .... district. He had been working for a (3) .... of stockbrokers called Coxon and Woodhouse, but unfortunately it lost a lot of money on the (4) .... and crashed, leaving Hall Pycroft and his (5) .... out of work.

Hall Pycroft (6) .... for a job with Mawson's, a company which (7) .... in valuable (8) .... However, he did not start this job because he met Mr Pinner, who asked him about the day's prices for the (9) .... of different companies and offered Hall Pycroft a better job as the business (10) .... for the Franco-Midland Hardware Company.

Useful Phrases

Match a verb with a noun/noun phrase to make phrases from the story. Then use the phrases to complete the gaps. You may need to change the form of the verb.

Verb	Noun / noun phrase
1 break	the worst
2 break off	trouble
3 fear	his time
4 do	his duty
5 make	her engagement
6 have	his mother's heart
7 take	his own way
8 waste	revenge

1 John McFarlane was worried that if the police charged him with murder, the scandal would *break his mother's heart*, so he asked Holmes to help him.

2 The police were not sure if the burnt flesh they had found was Mr Oldacre's, but they ....

3 Lestrade's telegram advised Holmes not to .... on McFarlane's case because new evidence proved he was guilty.

4 When McFarlane's mother discovered the man she was going to marry was not a good man, she had .... to him.

5 Oldacre wanted McFarlane to be found guilty of murder because he wanted to .... on Mrs McFarlane for not marrying him many years before.

6 When Holmes asked to know the content of the secret letter, the Prime Minister started to become angry and Holmes saw it was unusual for him not to ....

7 The two ministers were worried that if the letter was published, it would .... for the country and endanger peace in Europe.

8 When Holmes, dressed as a groom, was asked to witness a marriage, he .... and agreed.

Grammar: Active/passive forms

Choose the correct verb form, active or passive, to complete the sentences.

1 The Minister explained / was explained that an important document had disappeared / had been disappeared from his dispatch box.

2 The letter wrote / was written by the ruler of another country, who thought / was thought that British policy was a danger to his country.

3 Holmes read / was read in the newspaper that Lucas had murdered / had been murdered the previous night in his house.

4 The beautiful woman asked / was asked to see the room where the murder had happened / had been happened, and the policeman allowed / was allowed her to go into the room.

5 Lucas stabbed / was stabbed because Madame Fournaye believed / was believed she had caught / had been caught him with his other wife.

6 Holmes knew / was known that the carpet had moved / had been moved because the blood stain on the wooden floor was in a different place.

7 'Your husband's career and reputation will ruin / will be ruined if the letter doesn't find / isn't found,' said Holmes to Lady Hilda.

8 A wax impression of the dispatch box key made / was made by Lady Hilda.

Grammar: Past modal verbs of deduction

Write sentences using *must have, can't have* or *could have* to make deductions from the evidence given.

1 The bloodstained fingerprint on the wall proved that McFarlane definitely killed Oldacre.
McFarlane .... *must have killed Oldacre*.

2 The only way for Oldacre to get a copy of McFarlane's fingerprint was to ask him to press his finger into some wax to seal a letter.
Oldacre ....

3 It was not possible for Oldacre to carry out his plan alone without the help of his housekeeper.
Oldacre's housekeeper ....

4 We cannot be sure, but it is possible that the pieces of burnt flesh came from rabbits.
The pieces of burnt flesh ....

5 John Mitton was with friends on the other side of London when Lucas was killed, so it is impossible that he was the murderer.
John Mitton ....

6 Lady Hilda was the only person who was able to take the letter, because the dispatch box was kept in their bedroom.
No one except Lady Hilda ....

7 It is impossible that the servants took the letter. They did not know it was there, and the Minster trusted them completely.
The servants ....

8 The reason Mr Pinner asked Hall Pycroft to write the letter was surely so that his brother could later forge his handwriting.
Pinner ....

Grammar: Direct and indirect speech

Change the sentences from direct to indirect speech.

1 'I have travelled secretly from Prague to consult you,' said the king to Holmes.
The king told Holmes he *had travelled secretly from Prague Prague to consult him*.

2 'We will keep your secret,' said Holmes to the king.
Holmes told they king that they ....

....

3 'Is Irene Adler your legal wife?' Holmes asked the king.
Holmes asked the king ....

....

4 'Have you tried to buy the photograph back?' asked Holmes.
Holmes asked the king ....

....

5 'I'm getting married. And I can't get married without a witness,' said Mr Norton.
Mr Norton said that he ....

....

6 'Why hasn't Miss Adler made the photograph public already?' Holmes asked the king.
Holmes asked the king ....

....

7 'I'm sure I've heard that voice before,' said Holmes.
Holmes said that he ....

....

8 'I won't make the photograph public unless the king tries to make trouble for me,' said Irene.
Irene said that she ....

....

Making Questions

Write questions for the answers given. Use the first sentence to help you.

1 Mr Trelawney Hope lived in Whitehall Terrace.
Where did Mr Trelawney Hope live ? Whitehall Terrace
Who lived in Whitehall Terrace ? Mr Trelawney Hope

2 His dispatch box was kept on a small table beside his bed.
....? On a small table beside his bed
....? His dispatch box

3 The dispatch box was unguarded for four hours.
....? For four hours
....? The dispatch box

4 The foreign ruler was worried about British policy.
....? British policy
....? The foreign ruler who had written the letter

5 Madame Fournaye murdered Edward Lucas because she was angry and jealous.

....? Madame Fournaye

....? Edward Lucas

....? Because she was angry and jealous

6 Holmes showed the policeman a photograph of Lady Hilda.

....? Holmes

....? A photograph of Lady Hilda

....? The policeman

Macmillan Education
4 Crinan Street
London N1 9XW
A division of Macmillan Publishers Limited
Companies and representatives throughout the world

ISBN 978–0–230–43645–9
ISBN 978–0–230–43646–6 (with CD edition)

These versions of *The Norwood Builder*, *The Second Stain*, *The Stockbroker's Clerk* and *A Scandal in Bohemia* were retold by F H Cornish for Macmillan Readers.

First published 2013

Designed by Carolyn Gibson
Illustrated by Vіçtor Tavares
Cover photograph by Alamy/Finnbarr Webster. Sculpture by Mr John Doubleday.

Printed and bound by CPI Group (UK) Ltd, Croydon

without CD edition
2019 2018 2017
10 9 8 7 6 5 4 3 2

with CD edition
2019 2018 2017 2016 2015 2014
10 9 8 7 6 5 4 3 2